KING ARTHUR
AND HIS KNIGHTS
IN MYTHOLOGY

Evelyn Wolfson

 Enslow Publishers, Inc.

40 Industrial Road	PO Box 38
Box 398	Aldershot
Berkeley Heights, NJ 07922	Hants GU12 6BP
USA	UK

http://www.enslow.com

To Dacia, John, and Thea

Library of Congress Cataloging-in-Publication Data

Wolfson, Evelyn.
    King Arthur and His Knights in Mythology / Evelyn Wolfson.
       p. cm. — (Mythology)
    Includes bibliographical references and index.
    Summary: Examines both legend and historical fact surrounding King
Arthur and the Dark Ages in the British Isles.
    ISBN 0-7660-1914-4 (hardcover)
    Arthur, King—Juvenile literature. 2. Britons—Kings and rulers—Juvenile
literature. 3. Great Britain—History—To 1066—Juvenile literature. 4. Great
Britain—Antiquities, Celtic—Juvenile literature. 5. Arthurian romances—
Juvenile literature. [1. Arthur, King. 2. Arthur, King—Legends. 3. Kings,
queens, rulers, etc. 4. Great Britain—History—To 1066.] I. Title. II. Mythology
(Berkeley Heights, N.J.)
DA152.5.A7 W65 2002
942.01'4—dc21   2001004991

To Our Readers: We have done our best to make sure all Internet addresses in
this book were active and appropriate when we went to press. However, the
author and publisher have no control over and assume no liability for the
material available on those Internet sites or on other Web sites they may link to.
Any comments or suggestions can be sent by e-mail to Comments@enslow.com
or to the address on the back cover.

Cover and Illustrations by William Sauts Bock

CONTENTS

ACKNOWLEDGMENTS

My sincere thanks and appreciation for their advice, criticism, and comments to: Dorothy Tweer, Dacia Callen, and to my British friend Ann Williams, who grew up in the land of King Arthur knowing and loving Arthurian mythology.

PREFACE

During the Dark Ages, Britain was without a king and the country was divided. Death and destruction reigned over the land as power-hungry overlords armed themselves and fought against their fellow countrymen. Then, out of those dark and violent centuries, a legendary king arose and the people rejoiced. King Arthur brought peace and justice to Britain.

Historians are undecided about whether or not there was ever a hero named Arthur. If there had been, he would have lived in an Iron Age hill fort sometime during the fifth or sixth century and he would have been a soldier, not a king.[1]

But medieval audiences imagined that Arthur, his gallant knights, and Camelot existed in their own time period, not seven or eight centuries earlier.[2] The legendary King Arthur who reigned somewhere in between the twelfth and the fifteenth centuries became one of the most famous figures in British literature. Audiences imagined that King Arthur, his knights, and their ladies lived in a picturesque castle at Camelot, where they enjoyed sumptuous banquets, drank fine wine, dressed in elegant clothing, and enjoyed the fellowship of the Knights of the Round Table. *This* imaginary Camelot consisted of a castle surrounded by a town. It may have been located at Winchester, Caerleon, Carlisle, or Cardigan.

Historical Record

Barbarian invaders burned most of England's Roman records and almost nothing was recorded between the end of Roman rule in A.D. 410 and the appearance of Saxon kingdoms in A.D. 600—the time during which Arthur would have been king. Thus, most historical data have been reconstructed with a lot of guesswork. From the bits and pieces of materials that have survived, it has been determined that a British soldier named Arthur fought in a series of wars against nomadic invaders

Map of King Arthur's World

ORKNEY

Vikings
Angles
Saxons
Jut

Picts

Scotland
Scots

North Sea

Roman Antonine Wall

NORTHUMBRIA

Roman Wall of Hadrian

Ireland

CARLISLE

Isle of Man

FOUR POSSIBLE SITES OF CAMELOT

Irish Sea

YORK ((Roman Fort))

CHESTER ((Roman Fort))

CARDIGAN

Wales

MERCIA

NORFOL

CAERLEON ((Roman Fort))

England (Angeland)

Atlantic Ocean

WESSEX

LONDON
GLASTONBURY
WINCHESTER
CANTERBURY
KENT

WHER VIKIN LAND

TINTAGEL
CORNWALL
DORSET

English Channel

France

N
W · E
S

––––––– = Roman Roads

who assailed Britain after Rome withdrew her legions. Arthur's greatest victory was believed to have been the Battle of Badon Hill in southern England and was perhaps fought in Dorset.[3]

Thereafter, Britons enjoyed over a half-century of peace under Arthur's leadership. To maintain the peace, however, Arthur had to fight a number of battles against rebellious British kings.

Where the scanty bits of historical material left off, medieval storytellers began to create the King Arthur we know today: a great legendary hero with a plan for a new society. One of Arthur's strategies for maintaining peace was to allow defeated kings to retain their titles and dominance over their lands after they had sworn allegiance to him. Defeated kings were also invited to join Arthur's court at Camelot. King Pellinore, King Uriens, and other kings who served Arthur at Camelot also kept their titles and they appear in many of the Arthurian legends. King Lot of Orkney, who married Arthur's half-sister Morgause, stayed in northern Britain after his defeat, but his four sons (Gawain, Agravaine, Gaheris, and Gareth) joined Arthur at Camelot.

Another strategy attributed to Arthur's peace plan was the ideal of the Round Table. The Round Table symbolized Arthur's fellowship of knights and granted equal status to every knight who sat around the table. Arthur established a code of behavior for his knights that would exemplify proper conduct for all men everywhere. Knights of the Round Table would be expected to practice chivalrous behavior, meaning that they would defend people who were being cruelly treated (especially women), be virtuous, and never fail in their oath to the king.

The round table itself was a huge wooden circle that was surrounded by 150 tall chairs. Like place cards on a contemporary dining table, the backs of the chairs were inscribed with the names of each knight in gold letters: Sir Lancelot, Sir Gawain, Sir Bors, Sir Balyn, Sir Kay, Sir Launfal, Sir Agravaine, Sir Galahad, Sir Gaheris, Sir Gareth, Sir Percival,

Sir Tristan, and on and on around the table. When a new knight joined the Round Table, his name magically appeared on the back of a chair. And when a knight died, his name magically disappeared from the chair. One chair, inscribed on the back with the words *Siege Perilous*, remained empty for many years. (*Siege* is the French word for "seat.") It was reserved for the knight who would become the purest and most honorable knight in the world. But if the Siege Perilous was taken by a less deserving knight, it would go up in flames.

History

The Roman conquest of Britain occupied most of the first century A.D., beginning in the south and eventually including all of Britain up to a line between Carlisle and York. Attempts were made to conquer Scotland, but Rome never succeeded in holding the north. Wherever they conquered, the Romans built forts to control the countryside. Their remains can still be seen at Caerleon and elsewhere.

For three centuries, southern Britain enjoyed great prosperity under the paternal rule of the Roman Empire. London and the more prosperous cities of the region became cultural hubs where affluent citizens built fine homes and tried to emulate the elegance of Rome. In the countryside, landowners built villas and became wealthy using the labor of serfs, or slaves.

By the fourth century, however, the Roman Empire had begun to disintegrate and Rome started to withdraw her legions from England. Waiting to attack like wounded boars, the Picts and Scots began to strike from the north. They were joined by Anglos, Saxons, and Jutes (closely akin and often collectively called Saxons), who attacked from across the North Sea.

The Saxons landed along the east coast of Britain from Norfolk to Kent. They sailed up the island's rivers and traveled along Roman roads sacking and burning towns along the way. Many Britons were killed or taken prisoners. Others took their Roman culture, Christian religion, and language and fled to Cornwall, Wales, and Brittany.

Even before the Romans left Britain in the early fifth century, the British had already named a soldier, Constantine, as their own emperor. According to legend, Constantine had three sons: Constans, Aurelius Ambrosius, and Uther Pendragon. After Constantine's death, his son Constans became king. But Constans was murdered and his brother Aurelius Ambrosius took his place. Ambrosius successfully drove many of the Saxons out of Britain before he died [4]

During the same period, a power-hungry Britain named Vortigern came into power in Wales. Vortigern could not raise an adequate army to fend off invaders from the north, so he invited Saxons to come and settle in Britain and help him to defend the land. The Saxons arrived in droves and, eventually, Vortigern was replaced by the Saxon leader, Hengist.

During the fifth century, another leader, possibly Arthur, appeared on the scene and organized forces to fight against Hengist and the Saxon chiefs who succeeded him. Arthur, a formidable foe, stopped the Saxon advance and confined them to lands in the south and east. After his death, however, the Saxons returned in even greater numbers. Without a leader to stop them, they overran the rest of the country. The Saxons later called England "Angleland," and eventually became the English people.

By the sixth century, Roman civilization had been destroyed in Britain. Only roads and a few broken city walls remained. A number of petty kingdoms arose and leaders fought to either expand their holdings or defend what they held. Eventually, small kingdoms began to merge into larger ones. Northumbria became a northern kingdom, Mercia became a kingdom of the midlands, and Wessex became a southern kingdom.

In A.D. 597, Pope Gregory sent a monk named Saint Augustine to Kent. Augustine converted King Ethelbert of Wessex to Christianity, making the king the first Archbishop of Canterbury. Celtic Christianity had been practiced in England for three hundred years before Saint Augustine introduced Roman Christianity, and eventually a choice had to be made between the two. In A.D. 664, a council of bishops assembled in Kent, and Roman Christianity was chosen as the formal religion of Britain. Thereafter, Britain was organized into dioceses that provided needed unity for the country.

The legendary King Arthur reigned during the period of Roman Christianity in Britain. He was married to Queen Guinevere by one of the first Archbishops of Canterbury.

Between the seventh and ninth centuries, power shifted back and forth among Britain's three major kingdoms. Finally, King Egbert of Wessex declared himself king of all Britain in the early ninth century and his heirs ruled until the Norman conquest in 1066. Thereafter, Britain slowly emerged out of the Dark Ages of post-Roman rule and into the Middle Ages.[5]

Medieval Life

The medieval period, also called the Middle Ages, was rich with pageantry, mock wars, love, and adventure. The color and excitement of court life made up for the cold stone castles that the nobility called home during the eleventh and early twelfth centuries. Even after manor houses replaced castles, noblemen still built shallow-water moats around their homes and replicated grand dining halls inside. The gap between the British nobility and the British peasant was greater during the Middle Ages than during any other period in the country's history. Nobles flaunted their wealth by serving sumptuous banquets, wearing expensive clothing, and by living in large castles. The disparity between castle dining halls and country kitchens was most apparent. Arthur and his knights enjoyed an endless supply of wild venison, vegetables, breads, and wine. The peasants ate vegetables and porridge and drank weak beer. If they were fortunate enough to work for nobility or know someone who did, they might have enjoyed the nobles' leftovers.

The clothing worn by the two classes was also very different. Women of nobility wore fine silk undergarments covered by long silk dresses interlaced with threads of gold. Often, dresses were trimmed with ermine along the cuffs and collar or decorated with large, brightly colored gemstones. Men wore linen undergarments, tight pants, and richly colored wool or velvet tunics or doublets. Peasants wore plain linen tunics tied about the waist with rough cordage.

During the Middle Ages, powerful lords, barons, and kings employed knights, a term taken from an Anglo-Saxon word that meant "household warrior." At first, knights wore simple tunics, fought on foot, and carried clubs and axes. After the nobility began to fight on horseback, they wore heavy steel armor and carried lances, swords and shields. The extra sixty to eighty pounds of heavy armor made it impossible to mount their horses. Two servants had to help them up and hand them their weapons. As armor became increasingly elaborate, horses had to be specially bred to carry the extra weight. But heavy armor was a necessary means of protection for medieval knights because they had to defend themselves against opponents who carried the same types of wooden lances, shields, and swords.

The training for knighthood became a sophisticated affair. Many young men who aspired to knighthood apprenticed as a squire for eight or more years before becoming a knight. During training, a squire would serve an accomplished knight and develop skills as a horseman, archer, swordsman, and hunter. Squires studied the rules for chivalrous behavior and courtly love, but they had to wait until they became knights before they could practice at court what they had learned.[6]

Upon being knighted, squires took vows to be virtuous and never to break their code of chivalry or fail in their allegiance to their king. Sometimes, squires were knighted in a solemn church ceremony. But any knight could grant knighthood to a squire by simply tapping him on both shoulders with his sword and saying, "I dub thee knight."

A strict code of behavior was required for knights during duels, even when the battle was a fight for life. For example, men who agreed to fight had to wait at a distance from one another across a broad field. After both men were ready, they charged forward carrying blunt lances in one hand and shields in the other hand. The object of the lance attack was to unseat the opponent. After a man had dislodged his opponent from his horse, it was considered honorable to dismount and face his opponent on equal grounds before attacking with his sword. If a knight was fortunate enough to fall off his horse in just the right way, he could get up and fight. But if he had landed on his back, his heavy armor would have held him in place and he would be like an upside down beetle unable to turn over. Then his opponent might chuckle, help the poor man to get up, and say, "Jolly good round, old boy."

Courtly love was not an ideal in historical Arthur's time, but it appealed to Arthurian romance writers because it added spice to their stories. During the twelfth century, Andreas Cappellanus, a French monk, wrote *Handbook for Lovers*, which offered guidelines for the behavior of knights at court. Cappellanus' book included a long list of rules for courtly love, in which he affirmed that love and marriage were incompatible. He contended that, in order to experience real love, a man had to fall in love with someone else's wife. Sometimes the man worshipped her from afar, and sometimes they engaged in an affair. The affair between Lancelot and Guinevere was an example of courtly love.[7]

Medieval Storytellers

Between wars, British nobility enjoyed relative prosperity. Wealthy patrons supported artists and writers who composed entertaining works of fictional prose and poetry. People believed in magic, and that heaven and hell were physical places, so they had no trouble accepting that wizards, sorceresses, and fairies existed.

Some of the earliest bits of historical information about the time of Arthur appeared in a sermon titled "Concerning the Ruin of Britain," written by a Roman monk named Gildas during the middle of the sixth century. In the process of berating the British princes for their bad behavior, Gildas included a great deal of historical information, even though it did not include reference to anyone named Arthur. [8]

Welsh bards were popular entertainers from the eleventh century until the end of the thirteenth century, and many of their songs were based on historical incidents or happenings. As direct descendants of the Britons of post-Roman Britain, Welsh bards kept much of their folk tradition alive in their songs. Some of these songs have been preserved in a collection of Welsh tales called *The Mabinogion.* [9]

In A.D. 1136, Geoffrey of Monmouth, a Welsh scholar, wrote *History of the Kings of Britain*, which was based upon oral tradition and contemporary documents. In this book, the biography of a fictitious king named Arthur was created. But he did not become a popular mythical figure for another 300 years. [10]

In A.D. 1470, a Yorkist knight named Sir Thomas Malory composed a romance in English that told the full story of King Arthur and his knights. Malory was serving a prison sentence when he wrote *Le Morte d'Arthur* (*The Death of Arthur*); he had been accused of rape, theft, extortion, and attempted murder. But before he was imprisoned, he had read Geoffrey of Monmouth's *History of the Kings of Britain* and many of the French storytellers who had created Arthurian myths of their own. Malory, a gifted storyteller, had a strong sense of drama and was able to combine and adapt these earlier sources to create an exciting story. He brought the mythical king to life, and *The Death of Arthur* became an immediate literary success. Malory's work became the standard for the next 500 years. It inspired British and European writers to compose many more Arthurian myths. Later writers often changed the roles that Arthur and his knights played in their stories. They also changed the genealogy of the characters and created their own sequences of events. The hero who achieves the Holy Grail in Arthurian legends, for example, has been variously cited as Percival, Gawain, and Bors. In time, Arthurian myths and legends came to share only their medieval settings. [11]

Stories in this Book

With a few exceptions, most of the stories in this book have been taken directly from Malory's *Le Morte d' Arthur* (*The Death of Arthur*) (1470). "Percival" and "Lancelot and Guinevere" were taken from Chrétien de Troyes (1160–80). "Galahad" was taken from *The Vulgate Cycle* (1215–35), a collection of stories created by an anonymous author, and "Gawain and the Green Knight" was taken from the translation of a poem written by an anonymous fourteenth-century poet. Preceding each story is an introduction that gives the story's source and some background on the Arthurian character or characters in the story.

Today

In addition to literature, stories about King Arthur have influenced drama and art throughout the centuries. Medieval manuscripts contained interpretations of the legend and woodcuts used to illustrate Arthurian myths appeared in books as early as 1465. Although most tapestries depicting Arthurian scenes have not survived, those that have survived were woven in the 1300s. Tiles, murals, and mosaics were created throughout Europe depicting Arthurian subjects as early as the 1100s. Likewise, Arthurian characters and themes appeared in sculptures, carvings, and stained glass windows in England and Europe during the fifteenth century.

The British historian Geoffrey Ashe claims that there are now a hundred and sixty different Arthurian sites to visit in Britain, but only three really great ones: "Tintagel, the birthplace of Arthur, Cadbury, the possible residence, and Glastonbury, the death place."[12]

The Arthur who was a British soldier during the fifth and sixth centuries died in A.D. 542 near the River Camel in Cornwall after the Battle of Camlann.[13] But the legendary King Arthur who reigned during the Middle Ages lives on in stories, musicals, movies, and in the hearts and minds of people all over the world.

1

YOUNG ARTHUR

INTRODUCTION

During the fifth century, Uther Pendragon succeeded his brother Ambrosius Aurelius as king of Britain. Ambrosius had driven many of the Saxons out of Britain during his reign, but he had not freed Cornwall in southwestern England, and Pendragon made the defeat of the Saxons in that region a priority after his brother's death.

The Cornish peninsula is bounded on the south by the English Channel and on the north and west by the Atlantic Ocean. The coastline has high rocky cliffs that defended against an invasion from the sea. In addition, the windswept beauty of the moorlands and the mild moist climate along the coast had caused Pendragon to fall in love with the region long before he became king.[1]

Shortly after Pendragon had assumed the throne, the wizard Merlyn arranged for the king to spend the night with the wife of the Duke of Cornwall, Duchess Igraine, whom Pendragon desired. As a result of their union, a son was born and Merlyn took the boy away with him as payment for his magic.[2]

Early British historians could never document the connection between Cornwall and the birth of King Arthur. But storytellers solved the problem by resorting to the wizardry of Merlyn, who arranged for Arthur to be born at Tintagel. Merlyn made Arthur the chosen successor of Uther Pendragon, King of Britain, and permanently connected Arthur and Cornwall through their stories.

Merlyn was one of the most important characters in Arthurian myths and legends. According to T. H. White, he lived "backward in time," which means that he had already lived in the future. This enabled him to foretell events before they happened. Merlyn, whose father was believed to have been the devil, was captured when he was just a boy by the evil leader Vortigern. Vortigern's astrologers had predicted that the tower Vortigern was building to protect himself from

attack by Uther Pendragon would continue to collapse until the tower's mortar had been mixed with the blood of a fatherless boy. Because Merlyn's father was unknown, he seemed to be the answer to Vortigern's riddle. Vortigern had Merlyn captured and brought to him, but the young wizard told the power-hungry leader that the tower he was building kept collapsing because there was water beneath its foundation. He also said that there were two dragons in the water fighting against each other—a red one that represented Vortigern, and a white one that represented Uther Pendragon. Merlyn prophesied that the white dragon would kill the red dragon. Then the wizard disappeared before Vortigern could have him killed.

Merlyn did not reappear again in the story until many years later, after Uther Pendragon had indeed slain Vortigern. By then, Merlyn had become Pendragon's advisor. Merlyn arranged for the birth of Arthur and stayed with Arthur for most of his life.

Merlyn's education of young Arthur included lessons learned from a close relationship with the animal kingdom as well as the more worldly skills of jousting, horsemanship, and fencing. By the time Arthur was ready to take his rightful place on the throne, he was already prepared to implement his dream to create a perfect society.[3]

YOUNG ARTHUR

The King of Britain, Uther Pendragon, stood close to the blazing fire trying to warm his hands. The sun shone brightly outside but it never warmed the huge stone walls of the castle and the king was always cold. The king had recently returned home after a long battle against a large army of invading barbarians. Entertaining friends was his favorite means of leisure and King Pendragon awaited the arrival of a dozen weekend guests. The king had never married and he enjoyed surrounding himself with attractive women, including those who were already married. The beautiful and witty Dame Igraine, wife of Duke Gorlois from Cornwall, was one of Pendragon's favorite guests.

After the king's guests had arrived, they gathered in the castle's huge dining hall and toasted Pendragon's recent victories on the battlefield. Happy to be surrounded by so many friends, the king drank more wine than usual and paid Duchess Igraine more attention than was appropriate for a married woman.

By the end of the evening, Duchess Igraine was embarrassed and upset by the king's flirting. Deciding that the king had invited her to the castle to dishonor her, Duchess Igraine suggested to her husband, Gorlois, that they leave the castle during the night so that the king could not protest. After the festivities had ended and everyone had gone to their bed chambers, Duchess Igraine and her husband slipped away without being noticed.

The following morning, when the king discovered that Gorlois and Igraine had left the castle, he was furious. The couple's insulting behavior gave Pendragon a reason to declare war against Cornwall.

But Gorlois had anticipated trouble and he had already hidden his wife in the fortified castle of Tintagel on the north coast of Cornwall. The duke then returned to his stronghold at the castle of Terrabil about ten miles away. When Pendragon and his army of knights laid siege to the castle, the duke's forces quickly repulsed the attack. The fighting continued for many days and at last the king fell ill. Sir Ulfius, one of the king's most loyal knights, asked Pendragon what caused his illness, "I shall tell thee," said the king, "I am sick for anger and love of fair Igraine, that I may not be whole."[4]

Sir Ulfius was a kind and sympathetic knight and he did not like to see the king suffer. "I shall find the magician Merlyn," said Sir Ulfius, "and I shall ask him to work some of his magic for you." Sir Ulfius located the wizard sitting beside the road dressed as an old beggar. Ulfius explained to Merlyn that Pendragon's lovesick heart had taken hold of his body and that the King was unable to fight. Merlyn agreed to go with Sir Ulfius and assess the king's condition.

King Pendragon was so delighted to see Merlyn that he straightened up in his bed and the color returned briefly to his pale cheeks. Merlyn thought for a very long time before he spoke. "I shall bring you and Duchess Igraine together on the condition that the male child who shall result from your union be given to me to be raised." The king thought for almost an hour. His desire for the Duchess was so great, however, he finally agreed to Merlyn's condition.

Pendragon, Sir Ulfius, and Merlyn hastened to the castle of Tintagel where Duchess Igraine was in hiding. After the Duchess had retired to her bedchamber, Merlyn cast a spell that made King Pendragon resemble Duke Gorlois. Duchess

Igraine, believing that her husband had returned from battle, gladly welcomed him to her bed.

At the same hour that Pendragon came to Igraine, Gorlois was killed by King Pendragon's knights. Uther Pendragon waited an appropriate amount of time before asking the widow to marry him. "My three young daughters, Morgause, Elaine, and Morgan Le Fay, have lost their father," sighed Duchess Igraine, "I shall be pleased to be your queen."

The couple had a great wedding celebration and knights and their ladies came from all over Britain to honor the bride and groom. Then, less than nine months later, the new queen gave birth to a baby boy. Queen Igraine was delighted to finally have a son. But her joy was short lived. King Pendragon had to explain that it was he who had visited her at Tintagel castle while under a spell by the magician Merlyn. He confessed that he had also agreed to give the boy that would result from their union to Merlyn. Queen Igraine was overcome with shock and anger. Reeling from Pendragon's demand for her newborn son, she slapped, kicked, and spat out a stream of mean and nasty words in an uncontrollable fury. Pendragon protected his head from the queen's blows with his arms, but his ears could not shut out her angry words. When the queen had exhausted herself, she fell into a limp heap on the bed and sobbed most of the night.

King Pendragon remained silent. Finally, when dawn began to break, the queen sat up in bed and told the king that she would agree to honor his bargain with the wizard. Shortly thereafter Merlyn arrived and took the little boy to live with Sir Ector, his wife, and their son Kay in Wales.

Merlyn had arranged to leave the boy whom he called Arthur with Sir Ector and his family until the child was six years old. Then the wizard would return and take responsibility for Arthur's education. When Merlyn returned to Ector's castle, he offered to tutor the nobleman's son along with Arthur. Ector's son, Kay, was two years older than Arthur and extremely competitive, not too competent, and a braggart. He had only begrudgingly accepted his foster-brother and treated him like an unwanted guest. Kay constantly reminded Arthur that he would always be a squire because his parents were unknown. Arthur's happy open face never revealed the hurt that he felt.

Although Merlyn had agreed to educate both of the boys, his magic would only work with Arthur, so he kept it a secret from all the others. To satisfy Sir Ector's ideas about education, however, Merlyn scheduled several days a week during which the boys learned horsemanship, jousting, and chivalry. The rest of the week, he allowed Kay to entertain himself but sent Arthur on magical journeys throughout the animal kingdom. The wizard lived "backward in time" and never told the boy that he would grow up and become the king of England. And innocent young Arthur never asked Merlyn about his future. Arthur loved Merlyn deeply and trusted everything he said and did.

"What would you like to be today?" asked Merlyn, who was sitting with his back against an old oak tree. He wore a great silk robe trimmed in rabbit fur, and his long, curly mustache twisted down below his mouth and rested on the top of his silver-white beard. The little wizard's beard was so long it covered his chest and filled his lap.

Arthur shrugged his shoulders.

"Well," said Merlyn, "how about being a fish today? You could become a carp and go for a swim in the moat with the perches and pikes." Arthur agreed. But even after he had developed fins and gills, Arthur found it difficult to completely change his point of view. Over the years, however, the boy enjoyed many transformations.

Arthur had become obedient like an ant, wise like an owl, free like a wild goose, and clever like a badger. With each new experience, the boy learned important lessons about loyalty, responsibility, leadership, and humility—the character qualities necessary in a great king. Arthur enjoyed the fantasy world Merlyn created for him, but he also envied Kay, whose life was more normal. He wanted to become a knight like Kay someday. "Must I always be Kay's squire?" sighed Arthur. "I

want to become a knight, too." Arthur was idealistic, and the chivalrous life of a knight was very appealing to him.

Merlyn tried to humor the boy by making fun of knighthood. "It is a silly rule that a squire must know who is parents are," said Merlyn. "Don't envy Kay. He may be a knight some day, but he will never have crawled underground like an ant or a badger, and he will never have soared above the clouds like a wild goose."

Kay and Arthur were teenagers when the news that King Pendragon had died reached Sir Ector's castle. A messenger announced that the Archbishop of Canterbury had invited all knights and "gentlemen of arms"[5] to come to London, because the king had died leaving no heirs. But soon after Pendragon's death, a sword embedded in an anvil on top of a huge stone was found in London. The inscription on the stone offered the people of Britain a solution for finding the next king of England. It read: "Whoso pulleth out this sword of this stone and anvil, is rightwise king born of all England."[6]

The possibility of becoming king of England very much appealed to Kay. He insisted that his father take him to London. Arthur, who had become Kay's squire, dutifully followed his brother with childlike adoration.

Kay entered a jousting contest, but discovered that he had left his sword at the Inn where they had stayed the previous night. Kay directed Arthur to go back and get his sword. But when Arthur arrived at the Inn, it was locked up and everyone had gone off to the jousting competitions. Desperate to find a sword for his brother, Arthur ran wildly through the city until he stumbled upon a square where a large shiny sword stuck out from an anvil on top of a huge stone. The square was empty and Arthur could not ask to borrow the sword, so he pulled it out of the anvil and rushed to the jousting grounds to give it to his brother.

Kay immediately recognized the sword as the one that would be claimed by Britain's future king. "Look!" cried Kay to his father. "I have taken the sword from the stone."

Sir Ector's brow wrinkled as he looked at the sword that

Kay held up so proudly. The nobleman could see that it was indeed the magical sword that would make a man a king, but he doubted that his boastful son had removed it from the stone. "Shall we go to where the stone lays so that you can show me how you removed it?" asked Sir Ector. Reluctantly, Kay followed his father and Arthur back to the square. Sir Ector put the sword back into the anvil and asked his son to remove it. Kay struggled for some time but could not pull it out. Then, Sir Ector asked Arthur to try. The boy clutched the sword very gently and pulled it slowly toward him, as if it were only standing in a huge cake of cheese. Kay fell down on his knees and confessed to his father that it was Arthur who had brought him the sword. But Sir Ector was already kneeling before his foster-son. "Hail to the king. Hail to the king," said the very proud Ector.

Arthur was crowned at a great ceremony attended by huge crowds of cheering citizens and all the animals that had been his teachers. Sir Ector gave Arthur a tall cone with a light on top. When Arthur set the cone down on the table in front of him, it turned into Merlyn. The magician's eyes twinkled as he explained to the young king that Uther Pendragon had been his real father and that Merlyn had raised the boy knowing that some day he would be king of all Britain.

"I shall be with you for a long time," promised Merlyn. "And now, may I be the first to address you as King Arthur?" Then the crafty old magician shouted out the words, "King Arthur! King Arthur!" And a tear slipped down his cheek and disappeared into his long white mustache.

QUESTIONS AND ANSWERS

Q: *Explain why Duchess Igraine and the Duke of Cornwall left Pendragon's castle at night.*

A: Uther Pendragon had flirted with the duchess during dinner and Igraine believed the king's intentions were less than honorable. Fearing that the king would not allow them to leave, they slipped away during the night.

Q: *What was Merlyn's most important characteristic?*

A: Merlyn lived "backward in time," which gave him the gift of prophecy.

Q: *Describe the pact that Uther Pendragon made with Merlyn.*

A: In exchange for bringing Pendragon and Duchess Igraine together, Merlyn would receive the couple's unborn son.

Q: *Explain the importance of Merlyn's request to take Pendragon's son.*

A: Merlyn planned to raise a boy who would become a humane king with a plan for a new society.

Q: *Describe Merlyn's methods of educating young Arthur.*

A: Merlyn believed that he could teach Arthur important lessons in loyalty, responsibility, leadership, and humility by transforming him into a variety of animals.

Q: *Explain how Arthur ultimately became king of all Britain.*

A: After Pendragon died, Arthur went to London with Sir Ector and Kay. There, they found a sword that had magically appeared embedded in an anvil on top of a large stone. Arthur was the only person able to remove the sword from the stone, which proved him to be the future king of England.

EXPERT COMMENTARY

In *The Arthurian Legends*, editor Richard Barber gives his reasons for believing that King Arthur was a Welshman:

> This [King Arthur's] magical and mysterious world is founded on the figure of an obscure Welsh princeling, about whom we know nothing for certain. Arthur may have been the last Roman general of Britain, the first of those Welsh guerrilla fighters who defied the English until well into the Middle Ages, or a northern prince from Scotland who was later adopted by the Welsh living in Wales.[7]

Arthurian scholar Phyllis Ann Karr found the secrecy surrounding Arthur's birth and the early years that he spent with Sir Ector's family in Wales questionable and perhaps unnecessary:

> . . . I cannot help but wonder why and how it should have been for the good of Arthur and the kingdom to raise the heir in such secrecy. Uther married Igraine soon after Gorlois' death that by the rules of the milieu Arthur should have been recognized easily as Uther's legal son and heir; at any rate, the whole explanation was accepted by enough of the kingdom to give Arthur a following when Merlin finally gave it years later.
>
> . . . If there had been a visible heir, a son known to be of Uther's marriage, would the child really have run a great risk of assassination, surrounded as he would have been by barons? Would not Igraine or some strong baron simply have been named regent until his majority?[8]

2

THE MAGICAL
SWORD EXCALIBUR

INTRODUCTION

Swords were highly prized as symbols of knighthood during the middle ages. They were treated as valuable possessions and were often given names of their own. In medieval romances, swords sometimes appeared magically embedded in stone and could only be removed by the hero of the story. The most famous sword was embedded in an iron anvil on the top of a huge stone that magically appeared in Britain after King Pendragon died. This sword was removed by Arthur, the future king of England.

Another magical sword, Excalibur, was given to Arthur by The Lady of the Lake after he became king. The Lady of the Lake may have been a Celtic lake divinity similar to the lake fairies in modern Welsh folklore. The Welsh name for Excalibur was "Caladvwlch," a word that is similar to the name of a sword borne by heroes in Irish legend.[1]

Excalibur had an ornate handle covered with precious stones and its scabbard, or holder, was also decorated with gemstones interlaced with bands of gold. After Arthur retrieved Excalibur from a mystical hand that held it up in the middle of a lake, the wizard Merlyn asked the young king how he felt about the gift.

> "Whether liketh you better," said Merlin, "the sword or the scabbard?"
>
> "Me liketh better the sword," Arthur replied.
>
> "Ye are more unwise," said Merlin, "for the scabbard is worth ten of the swords, for whiles ye have the scabbard upon you, ye shall never lose no blood, be ye never so sore wounded; therefore keep well the scabbard always with you."[2]

Excalibur and its magical scabbard saved Arthur's life many times during his reign and, before he died, the king had the magical sword returned to the lake from which he had retrieved it.[3]

THE MAGICAL SWORD EXCALIBUR

Arthur's responsibilities as king kept him very busy and he was seldom able to go hunting or questing with his knights. His only enjoyment was a beautiful little rose garden that he created outside the walls of the castle. One day when Arthur was pruning his roses, a young squire came riding breathlessly into Camelot. Arthur left the garden and followed the young man into the courtyard. The boy's face was flushed and his fingers were raw from gripping his horse's reins. His breath came in small gasps as he spoke, "Please, Sire," he said, "please help me. My master lays wounded in the forest." The young squire described a powerful knight who guarded a road that his master had wanted to travel. The knight, who called himself Pellinore, had struck down the young man's master when he tried to pass.

Pellinore was well-known at Camelot as a formidable fighter, but Arthur believed that he could reason with him. He volunteered to go talk with the cranky old defeated king. A squire brought Arthur his horse and they all set off to find Pellinore. They had not ridden far when the young squire stopped and would go no further. "I shall wait for you here," said the frightened young man.

Arthur and Merlyn continued down the road until they found Pellinore. The brazen old king sat upon his horse and grinned at the new arrivals. "I understand that you are blocking this road," said Arthur, his manner tempered by Pellinore's imposing stand.

"I am. And what are you going to do about it?"

Arthur tried to sound firm but not angry. He did not want to duel with Pellinore. "I want you to reconsider your position. I want you to allow people to pass this way."

"Well, you will have to force me," said Pellinore. He gripped his lance, turned his horse, and readied himself to charge at Arthur.

Reluctantly, Arthur prepared himself to meet Pellinore's challenge. The two men rode some distance apart and then charged at each other at full speed. Pellinore's lance broke in half when it struck Arthur's shoulder. And Arthur's lance broke when it struck Pellinore's shield. Still, the men rode

back to their ends of the field, turned around, and charged at each other a second time. This time, Pellinore shoved Arthur off his horse with the blunt end of his broken lance. Arthur tumbled onto the ground, rolled over, and got up onto his feet just as Pellinore came around again on his horse. Arthur drew his sword from its scabbard and waited for Pellinore to dismount. The king was not at all sure that Pellinore would get down from his horse and obey the rules of chivalry.

"I am indeed a better swordsman than you are," shouted Arthur. "Now get down here and fight."

Pellinore was slow to dismount but he knew that Merlyn was watching from the sidelines, and he did not want to anger the old wizard. Pellinore and Arthur fought for most of the morning. Neither man was willing to admit defeat even though the forest clearing was strewn with pieces of broken armor and there was blood all over the grass. Merlyn watched with amusement. Arthur was badly wounded but he would not give up, and old Pellinore was so exhausted he could barely pull himself up from the ground.

For a time, the two men lay in the grass panting and gasping for breath. When Merlyn inquired as to whether the match was over, they both got up and began to fight again. Then, quite suddenly, Arthur's sword broke into two stubby pieces. Pellinore rushed toward him, shouting, "Surrender or you shall die!" But Arthur grabbed Pellinore by the leg, pulled him onto the ground, and began pounding him with the broken end of his sword. Arthur's persistence angered Pellinore so much that his energy returned and he attacked Arthur with the strength of a young man. Pellinore quickly straddled Arthur's chest, tore off his helmet, and raised his long, shining sword over Arthur's head. But before Pellinore could deliver the fatal blow, Merlyn cast a spell over him and the weary victor fell sideways off Arthur's body and onto the ground.

"Oh, you should not have killed him," said Arthur.

"Do not worry," said Merlyn. "He is only in a deep sleep and will awaken soon enough."

After Arthur had caught his breath, Merlyn helped him onto his horse and they headed back toward Camelot. But Arthur was upset that he had broken his sword. "How shall I fight with a broken sword?" he asked Merlyn. "If we meet another challenger, I will surely be killed."

Merlyn assured the young king that he would find a better and more powerful sword than the one that he had just broken. Merlyn was always reassuring Arthur that everything would turn out for the best; Arthur could not understand how the old wizard knew such things. He remained silent.

The exhausted young king was enjoying the coolness of the forest when all of a sudden a stream of bright sunlight

came beaming through the trees. Arthur began to trot his horse slowly toward the source of the sunbeam. He came upon a lush green field and beyond it lay a clear gray-green lake. Although the sun shone brightly, a thick, mysterious mist hung over the surface of the water. Arthur was staring out over the water when he saw something rise out of the mist in the middle of the lake. It was a thin white hand holding a shining silver sword and an ornate scabbard covered with precious stones.

Arthur gasped in disbelief. "Look out there!" he exclaimed.

Merlyn smiled. "The sword is Excalibur," he said. "It is

yours. It will serve you forever. And the scabbard is enchanted."

Arthur did not understand what Merlyn was talking about. But he was being drawn into the water toward the shining sword. All at once, a female figure draped in a long, gauzy, white gown floated above the mist in front of Arthur. "I am the Lady of the Lake," whispered the ghostly woman, "and you may have Excalibur. But first you must do as I ask."

The Lady of the Lake instructed Arthur to get into her little barge that floated among the reeds at the edge of the shore and let it take him out toward the sword. Arthur made his way through the reeds until he found the barge. He climbed onto the boat and sat still as it drifted out into the middle of the lake. As soon as the barge stopped, Arthur reached out and gently took the sword and scabbard out of the mystical white hand. At once, the hand disappeared beneath the water. Arthur sat very still, waiting to see if he, too, would disappear.

When Arthur returned to shore, Merlyn was wearing a broad grin on his crafty old face. Arthur ran his fingers up and down the sharp edge of the sword. Like a blind man, his fingers tried to read the mythical pattern of stones on the sword's handle.

"And what do you think about the scabbard?" asked Merlyn.

"It is quite beautiful," sighed Arthur. "But the sword is both beautiful and useful."

"You must not be fooled," warned Merlyn. "It is true that the sword will prevent you from ever being killed, but this is not an ordinary scabbard. As long as you wear this scabbard, you will never lose a drop of blood—no matter how badly you are wounded."

Arthur could not believe his good fortune, although he wished he had met the Lady of the Lake before he had dueled with Pellinore. Arthur and Merlyn galloped home toward Camelot, eager to introduce Excalibur to the Knights of the Round Table.

QUESTIONS AND ANSWERS

Q: *Explain the importance of the magical sword Excalibur and its scabbard.*

A: Excalibur magically protected Arthur from being killed during battle. The scabbard prevented the king from ever bleeding to death from a wound.

Q: *What was the difference between Excalibur and the sword in the stone?*

A: Excalibur was a magical sword that protected Arthur during battle. The sword Arthur removed from the stone made him king of all Britain.

Q: *Why did King Arthur agree to talk with Pellinore?*

A: They king wanted a reason to quest and he believed he could talk sense with Pellinore.

Q: *Describe Arthur's confrontation with Pellinore.*

A: Pellinore refused to stop blocking the road and challenged King Arthur to a duel. The two men fought and when Pellinore was about to deal Arthur a fatal blow, Merlyn interceded and put Pellinore into a deep sleep.

Q: *Explain how Arthur got the magical sword Excalibur.*

A: After the duel between Arthur and Pellinore, the young king and the wizard Merlyn came upon a mist-shrouded lake. A white hand rose out of the middle of the lake holding a shining sword and a jewel-covered scabbard. The Lady of the Lake appeared out of the mist and instructed King Arthur to take her magical barge out to the middle of the lake and retrieve the sword and scabbard.

EXPERT COMMENTARY

Malory does not make it clear that the sword that Arthur drew from the stone and anvil was a different one than the one given to him by the Lady of the Lake. But Phyllis Ann Karr explains that Excalibur's scabbard proves that there had to be two different swords:

> The importance of the scabbard is an argument for making Excalibur the sword given by the Lady of the Lake, since it is more difficult to account for a scabbard belonging specifically to a sword that appeared sheathed in stone and anvil.[4]

Scholars Lacey and Ashe suggest that Excalibur was not thrown back in the lake but was given to Richard I.

> When Richard I visited Tancred of Sicily in 1191, he presented him with a sword that he claimed was Arthur's. It is not clear where it came from, but he was doubtless aware of the reported finding of Arthur's grave at Glastonbury, and he may have used this to 'sell' another relic. He would not have felt any inconsistency in producing the sword, because the story of its casting-away was not yet embodied in any literary version.[5]

3

MORGAN LE FAY

INTRODUCTION

Morgan Le Fay may have developed from the goddess Modron and appeared much later in Arthurian literature. She was named Morgan in Brittany, where there was a belief in a class of water-fairies called "Morgans." Her magical powers were extensive. Sir Thomas Malory (1470) recognized Morgan Le Fay's divine status and made her the half-sister of King Arthur. They shared the same mother, Duchess Igraine of Cornwall.[1]

After Morgan Le Fay's sisters grew up and got married, the eccentric little girl was sent to a nunnery to be educated. By the time she was old enough to leave the nunnery, Morgan had quite mysteriously learned a great deal of magic. She could cast spells, change shape, and make things disappear with the wave of a hand. But she could not make big things happen, like the way that Merlyn had brought about the birth of her half-brother Arthur.[2]

Morgan Le Fay took out her anger and frustration on Arthur and spent most of her life plotting to overthrow him. In many Arthurian tales, Morgan is depicted as an evil sorceress. But it was also said that after Arthur's last battle, Morgan carried him off in a boat to Avalon, a mythical island to the west, where she tended his wounds.

MORGAN LE FAY

The midday sun warmed the court at Camelot where the knights and their ladies gathered to plan their afternoon activities. Morgan Le Fay stood beside Arthur and feigned interest in the hawk he was tracking. "He is indeed beautiful," exclaimed Morgan as she watched the hawk soar high above the castle. Then, pretending to steady herself as she gazed up into the air, Morgan leaned on King Arthur's arm. Her long silk robe curled around his left side and covered Excalibur.

"A beauty. A real beauty," repeated Arthur without lowering his gaze. While Arthur stared up at the sky, Morgan used her skillful sorcery to exchange her brother's magical sword, Excalibur, for her lover's ordinary sword.

Gripping her silk robe so that Excalibur would remain well hidden, Morgan slipped away from her brother and hurried into the castle to find her lover, Sir Accolon. "Oh, my dear, handsome Accolon, how well you shall look in a gold crown," smirked Morgan as she breezed into Accolon's room. Morgan had finally found a lover brave enough to help her kill King Arthur. Poor Accolon did not know that he was smitten with an evil sorceress. He was willing to do anything Morgan asked of him.

"I have succeeded—the king has your sword and I have Excalibur for you," she said as she pulled the magic sword from under her robe. "After you have killed Arthur, I shall kill my husband. Then, you shall be the new king and I shall be

the new queen of Britain." A thin, sinister smile passed across Morgan's face as she kissed her naive lover on the cheek and flitted out of the room.

Morgan was so pleased with herself that she skipped like a young girl back to her chambers. The following morning, she sprang out of bed, anxious to see if the king and his knights had left to compete in a jousting tournament in Wales. She tiptoed to the window and saw that the courtyard below was quite empty. As usual, her husband, King Uriens, lay snoring in bed. Uriens, who was older and much less clever than his wife, was not fond of exercise. He had not entered a competition for many years.

Morgan crossed the room and removed her husband's sword from the wall hook. The sword was quite heavy and she needed to practice swinging it in the air. First, she stood in the middle of the room, raised the sword over her head, and whirled it around in great circles. After she got better at it, she went to the bed where her husband laid snoring and practiced whirling the sword over his head. "Oh, what a sweet song you sing," she whispered.

In the meantime, Sir Accolon had been late leaving Camelot because he had had to rummage through the castle storerooms and put together a suit of much-used armor that the king would not recognize. At last, he left the castle carrying a very dented shield and Excalibur covered over with a long black cloth.

At the jousting tournament, the young knight sought out the king and challenged him to a match. King Arthur did not recognize the stranger and when he asked his name, Accolon would not reveal it. Arthur agreed to joust anyway, and rode to the end of the field. Accolon turned and rode in the opposite direction. The two men shut their helmets and charged at each other at full speed. Arthur, who was a skilled horseman, knocked Accolon backward off his horse on the first pass. In the proper knightly fashion, the king dismounted his horse and drew his sword. Accolon smirked beneath his heavy metal helmet. With Excalibur in hand, he lashed out at the king, swinging the magical sword back and forth. Accolon broke pieces off Arthur's shield and then cut into the king's flesh through small openings in his armor. The king's wounds did not bleed because he still had the magical scabbard, but his sword felt weak and unresponsive. King Arthur fought until he could barely stand up. But just when the young stranger thought the king was defeated, Arthur suddenly lunged forward and delivered a crushing blow to the breast of the stranger. Accolon stumbled backward and lost his grip on Excalibur. It clattered to the ground.

Arthur gasped when he saw Excalibur lying on the ground beside him. "So, it was Excalibur that enabled you to fight so gallantly?" exclaimed Arthur as he raised the sword over the young man's head. "Who are you? And where did you get my sword?" demanded the king.

Sir Accolon begged for mercy. He confessed that it had been Morgan's plot to kill the king and Morgan's husband in order to take the throne. King Arthur relaxed his grip on Excalibur and let Accolon get up off the ground. He pitied the young man because he had come under one of Morgan's spells. "I forgive you," said the king, "and shall spare your life this one time. Now, go back to Camelot and tell my evil half-sister that the king lives."

Unaware that her lover had failed to kill the king, Morgan Le Fay prepared to carry out her side of the compact at Camelot. She tiptoed over to where he husband's sword hung on the wall and slipped it quietly off the hook. Just then, the door opened and Morgan's youngest handmaiden entered the room carrying a tray of hot tea. "Oh, my lady," whispered the startled girl, "I heard that you were up early and—" The maid stopped in her tracks when she saw Morgan holding her husband's sword. "Is anything wrong, my lady?" she asked, staring at the sword in Morgan's hand.

"No. Not at all," replied Morgan. "I was just putting this away." She walked back toward the wall where her husband's scabbard still hung.

The handmaiden curtsied, left the room and went directly

to Sir Uwaine's room. "Sire, Sire," she cried as she shook Morgan's son to awaken him. "Your mother may be doing something to hurt herself. She has your father's sword. Come quickly."

Uwaine hurried to his parents' room. When he entered, he saw his mother whirling his father's sword over the king's head. "Stop," exclaimed Uwaine. "Have you gone mad?"

Uwaine grabbed the sword out of his mother's hand and pushed her away from the bed. King Uriens continued to sleep soundly. Morgan was angry that her son had interfered and that she would have to devise another plan to kill her husband. She explained her scheme to Uwaine and promised him that he would gain much status once she and Accolon were queen and king. Uwaine's silence was agreement enough for his mother.

Later that day, a messenger returned to Camelot with the body of Morgan's lover draped over his horse. Accolon's wounds had been so severe that he had bled to death on the way home. The messenger asked to see Morgan Le Fay so that he could deliver the message from King Arthur. It read: "The king is alive and well and will return to Camelot."

Morgan Le Fay's whole body twisted in anger and disbelief when she saw her lover's lifeless body and heard that Arthur was still alive. Her evil eyes blazed with anger as she rubbed her hands together trying to come up with another plot. When she finally decided that she would have to find Arthur and take Excalibur herself, Morgan gave Guinevere a lame excuse for having to leave Camelot. She traveled for several days and finally found the nunnery where Arthur lay recuperating. In her sweetest and most convincing manner, Morgan persuaded the nuns to let her visit Arthur's room. "I am so worried for my brother," Morgan lied. "I must see him."

The old nuns were so touched by Morgan's devotion that they allowed her to visit her wounded brother. Fortunately, King Arthur slept with Excalibur gripped tightly in his right hand. But Excalibur's scabbard rested loosely against the bed. Morgan glided into the room, pretended concern, and after the nuns had left, she snatched up the scabbard and tucked it under her long cloak. Arthur did not awaken and after a reasonable amount of time, Morgan bade the nuns goodbye. "You are most kind to care for my dear brother," she said as she walked out of the door, clutching her cloak tightly about the neck.

Later that afternoon, Arthur woke up and discovered that his scabbard had disappeared. He shouted at the nuns and demanded that they tell him who had taken it. "I am sorry my king," said a small older nun clasping her hands nervously. "Only your beloved sister came to visit. She was most concerned about you. It could not have been she who took your scabbard."

Arthur fell back onto his pillow and sighed. Had Excalibur not been in his hand, Morgan would have taken that, too. Arthur waited until darkness covered the grounds of the nunnery and then slipped outside. He went directly to the stable, prepared his horse, and slipped away under the cover of night.

Arthur rode throughout the night and by morning had caught up with his evil half-sister and her small army of faithful soldiers. "Stop," cried Arthur. "Stop and return my scabbard." But Morgan raced her horse toward a large lake and threw the scabbard into the deepest part of the water. When Arthur reached the lake, Morgan had disappeared. He rode aimlessly into a broad valley strewn with large rocks and never recognized Morgan and her men lying on the ground in the form of ordinary stones.

Some time later, Morgan Le Fay returned to the castle that Arthur had given her in Gore, a kingdom bordering on Scotland. She waited several weeks, then sent a messenger to Camelot with a gift for Arthur. "Take this robe to my brother," said Morgan to her young messenger. "It holds great magic." The robe was made from bright green velvet and studded with precious emerald stones.

After the young messenger arrived at Camelot, she was

taken directly to the king. "Your sister, Morgan Le Fay, has sent me with this peace offering. She is most sorry that you were outwitted and lost your scabbard." The young girl handed the beautiful green robe to the king and stepped backward. But Nimue, Merlyn's apprentice wizard, warned the king that he should have Morgan's messenger try the robe on before he accepted it. "Please," said the king politely to the beautiful young woman who had handed him the robe, "model the robe for me?"

The young woman's eyes grew wide and she gasped for breath. "Oh, please, Sire," she protested, "this robe is only fit for a king. I cannot wear it." But Arthur insisted. The young girl began to sob. She did not know what magic Morgan had wrapped into the beautiful robe, but she knew that the magic Morgan worked on her brother was always harmful. The young girl hesitated, then she took the robe into her thin white hands and wrapped it ever so slowly around her shoulders. Whish! The robe and Morgan's young messenger went up in flames.

Arthur's anger flared as he stared at the small pile of ashes in front of him. Then he vowed before all the knights of the Round Table that he would never again welcome Morgan Le Fay back to Camelot.

QUESTIONS AND ANSWERS

Q: *What was Morgan Le Fay's relationship to King Arthur?*

A: She was Arthur's half-sister; their mother was Igraine.

Q: *What were Morgan Le Fay's most important characteristics?*

A: Arthur's half-sister was no ordinary mortal. Morgan was a sorceress who had the power to cast spells, change shape, and make things disappear with the wave of a hand.

Q: *Describe Morgan's plot to kill her husband, King Uriens, and her half-brother, King Arthur.*

A: Morgan stole King Arthur's magical sword, Excalibur, and gave it to her lover, Sir Accolon, to use to kill Arthur. Morgan would take responsibility for killing King Uriens. After both men were dead, Morgan and Sir Accolon would be the new queen and king.

Q: *Explain what happened in the duel between Sir Accolon and King Arthur.*

A: Sir Accolon dropped Excalibur during his duel with the king. After Arthur discovered that his evil half-sister had plotted against him, he spared Sir Accolon's life and sent him back to Camelot with the news that the king was alive and well.

Q: *Describe Morgan Le Fay's reaction after she learned that her plot had failed.*

A: She became furious upon seeing that her lover was dead and that King Arthur was still alive. She gave Queen Guinevere a weak excuse for having to leave Camelot and set out to find Arthur and steal Excalibur herself.

Q: *Did Morgan Le Fay succeed in taking Excalibur from Arthur?*

A: No. When Morgan found the nunnery where Arthur was recovering, she discovered that he held the magical sword in his hand while he slept. So she stole the scabbard that rested beside the king's bed, instead.

Q: *Did Arthur recover Excalibur's scabbard from Morgan?*

A: No. Morgan threw the scabbard into the middle of a lake, changed herself and her men into stones so that Arthur could not find them, and later returned to her castle in Gore.

Q: *Describe the gift Morgan sent to King Arthur as a "peace offering."*

A: Morgan sent Arthur a luxurious robe studded with emerald stones that was filled with her own brand of evil magic. When Morgan's messenger modeled the robe, it went up in flames and both robe and messenger were reduced to ashes.

EXPERT COMMENTARY

Phyllis Ann Karr remarks that Morgan took up residence in a variety of castles in England and took many lovers over the years:

> One conceives that she [Morgan] was eventually forced to vacate Gore rather than run afoul of her husband or his deputy King Bagdemagus. She owned, acquired, or usurped more than one castle outside Gore, from which she could operate.
>
> . . . She seems, however, to have had her lovers one at a time, taking a new one only some while after the former one was slain or otherwise lost.[3]

Morgan Le Fay has been portrayed as a fairy and a member of a sisterhood of healers. She has also been portrayed as an evil sorceress:

> Since medieval Christianity, unlike the earlier Celtic variety, had difficulty finding a place for a benign or neutral enchantress, Morgan tends to become more sinister, a witch taught by Merlin who applies her arts maliciously.
>
> . . . She is associated with art and culture, and despite all the scheming at the court it is still Morgan, with attendant ladies, who carries away the wounded King over the water to his Avalonian place of healing.[4]

4

GAWAIN AND THE GREEN KNIGHT

INTRODUCTION

An anonymous fourteenth century poet composed a long verse that had its origins in a similar ancient Irish narrative. Entitled "Gawain and the Green Knight," the poem was about one of the knights of the Round Table and was filled with suspense, adventure, and horror.[1]

Sir Gawain was one of four sons of Queen Morgause, Arthur's half-sister. Since kinship among medieval families required that an uncle afford his nephews special treatment, Gawain was made a knight at King Arthur's court. The king admired Gawain's loyalty, gallantry, and courage. And Gawain was fiercely protective of his uncle. Gawain seldom quested after duels with other knights, but preferred to rescue damsels in distress and to protect and save them from cruel treatment. His oath of chivalry ranked high in his code of behavior and he was well-known for his chivalrous deeds. Yet, he never shrank from a dangerous challenge.

King Arthur had established a holiday tradition at Camelot that included a sumptuous banquet, during which the Knights of the Round Table would recount their quests during the past year. At one Christmas celebration, however, an uninvited intruder entered the dining hall and presented King Arthur and the Knights of the Round Table with a horrifying challenge.

Sir Gawain volunteered to accept the challenge without fully understanding the consequences. Neither King Arthur nor his knights realized that the challenge presented to them had been concocted by the evil sorceress Morgan Le Fay. Arthur's evil half-sister had hoped to scare Queen Guinevere to death, and prove that there were no brave or noble knights among those who sat at the Round Table. But she failed on both counts.[2]

GAWAIN AND THE GREEN KNIGHT

King Arthur hosted festive holiday celebrations at Camelot and knights who had been questing always tried to return home for the merrymaking. The king hired minstrels to play and sing, and he arranged to have long wooden dining tables laden with platters of wild boar, turkey, and venison; bowls of fresh vegetables; and baskets of piping-hot bread. Throughout the meal, the Knights of the Round Table recounted their questing experiences, one at a time, and everyone toasted to their grand feats of chivalry.

One year, in the midst of a joyous Christmas celebration, the great doors of the dining hall flew open and a large green-colored man riding a huge green stallion galloped into the room. The minstrels stopped playing, the servants stopped serving, and the knights stopped eating. Everyone stared in amazement at the great, green man who wore no armor but rode like a knight. The Green Knight carried a large green axe in one hand and in the other hand held a green bough from a holly tree. The stranger's skin, beard, long hair, and clothing were various shades of green and his leather belt and saddle had bright emerald-green stones attached. The green-colored stranger rode boldly up to the table in front of the king and pulled his stallion to a halt.

Before Arthur could speak, the Green Knight threw the holly bough on the ground and shouted, "I have come by the peaceful sign of the holly bough to challenge the brave and

chivalrous Knights of the Round Table. If there is a brave knight among you, then shall he be brave enough to cut off my head with this axe? I require only that I have the right to deal my own blow, in my own way, one year from now."

The Knights of the Round Table, unwilling to make eye contact, looked down at their plates. After an awkward silence, King Arthur stood up and exclaimed, "I shall accept your challenge!"

Before the king could push back his chair, however, Sir Gawain jumped to his feet and declared, "Please, Sire, allow me."

A great grin spread across the Green Knight's face as he jumped down from his horse and strode to the middle of the hall. He handed his green axe to Gawain and commanded, "Take my axe and cut off my head." Then he knelt down, scooped his long green hair up from the back of his head, and tossed it forward to bare his neck. Gawain had not anticipated that the challenge would be so gruesome and he took a step backward. He stared at the large shiny axe that the Green Knight had placed in his hand and then down at the knight's bare neck.

"Are you not a brave Knight of the Round Table?" sneered the Green Knight. "Can you not take off my head?"

Gawain's white-knuckle grip on the axe handle grew tighter as he raised the sharp, shiny blade high over his head and brought it down on the eerie green neck of the stranger. Sparks flew as soon as the axe had cut through the flesh and bone and struck the hard stone floor. The Green Knight's head tumbled oddly across the floor, never breaking the silence that filled the room.

King Arthur and his knights gasped when the Green Knight straightened up his headless body and began to feel around the floor, looking for his head. When at last he found it, he picked it up, tucked it under one arm, and sprang up onto his horse. Then, he turned the head toward the table and it spoke:

> Gawain, be ready to ride as you promised;
> Hunt me well until you find me—
> As you swore to, here in this hall, heard
> By these knights. Find the green chapel, come
> To take what you've given, a quick and proper
> Greeting for a New Year's Day. Many men
> Know the knight of the green chapel:
> Seek me, and nothing can keep you from me.
> Then come! Or be called a coward forever.[3]

Then the green horse, carrying its headless green rider, galloped freely out of the hall and into the night.

A heavy silence hung over the great dining hall. Servants moved silently among the guests, filling dishes and replenishing drinks. The result of Sir Gawain's impulsively brave act had shocked and bewildered his fellow knights and it took some time before conversation and laughter resumed.

The remainder of the year passed very slowly for Sir Gawain. He did not go questing, but instead prepared himself for the dreadful adventure that awaited him. When at last the time came to find the green chapel, Sir Gawain bade goodbye to his king and queen and set off to South Wales. Unfortunately, Gawain's shiny silver shield with its five-pointed star of the Britons emblazoned in the center attracted men who longed to joust with a knight of King Arthur's court. As a result, Gawain had to respond to an endless number of challenges all along the way. Fortunately, Gawain fought valiantly and each time remained the victor. But the journey was tiresome, lonesome, and fearful. At night, robbers tried to steal his sword or his horse while he slept. During the day, the young knight often went hungry and thirsty. And nowhere along the way did he meet anyone who had heard of the green chapel.

Late one day, Gawain came upon a vast opening in the forest. Great oak trees dotted a soft valley of lush green grass that led up to a fine castle surrounded by a broad moat. Gawain had three days left to locate the green chapel and lose his young head. But he wanted very much to eat a hot meal and to sleep in a soft bed before he died. As he approached the edge of the moat, a cheery squire lowered the drawbridge and motioned Sir Gawain forward. The young knight rode into the castle courtyard, dismounted, and handed his horse's reins to the squire.

Inside the castle, Sir Gawain followed an ancient old lady, who cackled as she walked, into a large room where a fire burned brightly. A tall muscular man with rusty-red hair and a red face rose from his chair by the fireplace and greeted Sir Gawain. "What brings you to my castle?" he asked, smiling broadly.

Sir Gawain explained that he was on a quest to find the green chapel before New Year's Day but that no one could direct him to it. The lord of the castle, Bercilak de Hautdesert, smiled and clasped the young knight's hand. "The green chapel is but a two-hour ride away," he explained. "I shall have a squire take you there when the time has come. In the meantime, please stay as my guest."

At dinner that evening, the lady of the castle greeted Sir Gawain with much enthusiasm. She was a small, slim young woman with cold black eyes and shining jet-black hair that fell to her waist. She extended her hand to Gawain and he kissed it ever so lightly.

During dinner, Bercilak explained that he would be going hunting in the morning and would return by dinnertime. He assured Gawain that his wife and her handmaidens would take good care of him. "We shall strike a pact," said the lord of the castle. "I shall give you the best of the hunt each day in exchange for anything that you obtain here in the castle."

The men shook hands and everyone went off to bed. The following morning, Bercilak left early for the hunt and Gawain lingered in his soft, warm bed. Then, very quietly, the door to Gawain's room opened and the lady of the castle came in. She sauntered over to the bed, sat down beside Gawain, and coyly worked at smoothing out the wrinkles in her soft velvet dress.

"Does our gallant guest need a kiss before he rises?" she

asked. Without waiting for an answer, she leaned forward and Gawain gave her a quick kiss on the cheek. Then he pulled himself up into a seated position as quickly as possible to avoid her pursed lips. The lady laughed lightly and got up. "You are indeed a most chivalrous knight," she said, smiling. "But surely you don't find me unattractive?"

"Oh, no, my lady. You are most beautiful, indeed. But I am a Knight of the Round Table and I cannot kiss another man's wife."

The lady of the castle fluttered her eyelashes at the innocent young knight, smiled, and left the room.

When Bercilak came home that evening, he greeted Sir Gawain with a broad grin and handed him a fat turkey to fulfill his side of their bargain. "Thank you, Sire. I am most pleased," said Gawain.

"And what have you for me?" asked the lord of the castle. Sir Gawain laughed heartily, stepped in front of the lord, and kissed him on the cheek. "You have indeed pleased me well," said the lord. "Now we must drink to a good day."

The following morning after Bercilak had left to go hunting, his wife went once again to Gawain's room. This time, she knelt on the bed next to the young knight and gently brushed a lock of golden hair from his face. "A kiss today?" she whispered, leaning seductively toward Gawain's face. "Such a gallant knight may never visit our castle again."

Gawain was pinned down on the bed. To avoid her lips, he had to kiss first one cheek and then the other and quickly straighten up. "What sweet kisses," she mused. Then she walked to the door and smiled flirtatiously as she closed it behind her.

That evening when the lord of the castle returned home, he handed Gawain the head of a wild boar. In exchange, Gawain planted a kiss on each of the lord's cheeks. "I am indeed pleased with our exchange," said the lord. Once again, they all enjoyed an evening of good food and conversation.

"I regret that tomorrow is New Year's Day and I must leave," said Gawain, as he prepared to go to bed.

"Oh, but you must stay until after lunch," said Bercilak. "I shall come home for lunch and then my squire will lead you to the green chapel."

The following morning, after the lord had left to go hunting, the lady of the castle came once again to Gawain's room. This time, she tried even more aggressively to make him accept her overtures. Always the gentlemen, Gawain kissed her on both cheeks and then pulled away. He continued to assure her that he would be most interested in her kisses were she unmarried. In exasperation, the lady of the castle removed a small piece of green lace from her sleeve and handed it to Gawain. "Do not tell anyone that I have given this to you," she said, "but keep it with you, and you will live forever."

After she had left the room, Gawain tucked the little piece of green lace into his belt and got dressed. He would need all the help he could get to remain alive and the green lace offered him a bit of hope. Before lunch, Bercilak returned from the hunt and handed Gawain the antler of a young deer.

"And what have you for me in exchange?" asked the lord anxiously.

Gawain stepped forward and gave his host a kiss on both cheeks, but he did not reveal the green lace. After lunch, Gawain thanked his host and hostess and rode off into the forest with a young squire. Gawain believed it was a happy ending to his short life. By the time night came, his head would have been cut off and he would be dead.

At a clearing in the forest, the young squire stopped and pointed toward a large mound in the distance. "There is the green chapel," said the squire.

"That?" exclaimed Gawain. "That is a mound."

"It is also the green chapel," replied the squire. "But I would not go there if I were you. No one ever returns from there alive."

Gawain thanked the young squire and rode toward the

mound. As he approached, he heard the sound of grinding steel. Gawain's shirt was wet with perspiration and he wanted to turn around and gallop off. But he knew that it was too late to turn back. "Is anyone there?" he asked in a trembling voice.

Within seconds, the Green Knight, as large and as green as Gawain remembered him, came rumbling out the chapel door, holding a newly sharpened green axe. "So, you have come. Now I shall repay the stroke you dealt me at Camelot. Take off your helmet and stretch your neck out on that rock," he bellowed.

Gawain did as he was told and the Green Knight swung the axe back and forth in the air until it whistled. Gawain flinched when he heard the axe cutting through the air. But it did not strike the frightened young knight.

"So the brave Knight of the Round Table is scared," jeered the Green Knight. Gawain promised himself that he would not flinch a second time and begged the Green Knight to go ahead and strike the deathblow. The Green Knight made the axe whistle a second time over Gawain's head, but this time the young knight did not flinch. "So you are brave," sneered the Green Knight as he raised the axe overhead a third time. This time, the axe struck the side of Gawain's neck and blood dripped onto the ground. Gawain waited for his head to roll off the rock, but nothing happened.

"Get up," chuckled the Green Knight. "I am not going to cut off your head. You have fulfilled your part of the bargain." The Green Knight rested his sharp green axe against the rock and explained to Gawain that he and the lord of the castle were one and the same. He admitted that the ancient old lady who had led Gawain to the castle was actually Morgan Le Fay, and that it was she who wanted to determine the truth of the Round Table's fame.[4]

"My axe cut the air for the first kiss that you gave to my wife," he said. "And it cut the air the second time for the two kisses that you gave her. But I was forced to wound you with the third blow, not for the two kisses that you gave her, but because you did not reveal the green lace that she gave to you."

Gawain hung his head in shame. "Forgive me," he said.

"Oh, I have already forgiven you," said the Green Knight. "Had you yielded to dishonor and shame, your head would be rolling on the ground. You kept the green lace a secret in the hope that it would save your life, not for the love of another man's wife. I can understand that."

Gawain returned to Camelot and told his story to King Arthur and the Knights of the Round Table, who marveled at his chivalry and bravery. All agreed that not one among them was more worthy of knighthood that young Sir Gawain.

QUESTIONS AND ANSWERS

Q: *What was Gawain's relationship to King Arthur?*

A: Gawain was Arthur's nephew and the son of Queen Morgause, Arthur's half-sister.

Q: *What was the challenge that the Green Knight presented to the Knights of the Round Table?*

A: The Green Knight challenged one of the knights to cut off his head. In exchange, the Green Knight wanted to deal his own blow in his own way a year, at the green chapel in Wales.

Q: *How did Arthur and the Knights of the Round Table respond to the Green Knight's challenge?*

A: Arthur's knights kept their heads down and did not rise to the challenge. When Arthur volunteered, Gawain protested and stepped in and took the king's place.

Q: *Describe Gawain's experiences on his way to the green chapel.*

A: Gawain had to fight against men eager to duel with a Knight of the Round Table, stay awake at night to protect himself against robbers, and go hungry. After he accepted the hospitality of a kind lord and lady, he had to rebuke the advances of the lady of the castle.

Q: *What was the pact that the lord of the castle made with Gawain?*

A: The lord of the castle offered to give Gawain the fruits of his daily hunt in exchange for whatever Gawain had received during the day from the lady of the castle and her handmaidens.

Q: What was the lady of the castle's purpose in trying to seduce young Gawain?

A: The lady of the castle was testing Gawain's chivalry to see if he would commit adultery. But Gawain only gave her kisses on the cheek.

Q: What happened after Gawain finally arrived at the green chapel and found the Green Knight?

A: The Green Knight pretended that he was going to cut off Gawain's head but only swung the axe in the air twice and made a small cut the third time.

Q: Identify the Green Knight. What was the purpose of his challenge?

A: The Green Knight and the lord of the castle were one and the same. The lord of the castle had tried to prove that there were no noble knights of the Round Table. Had Gawain yielded to dishonor and shame, Morgan Le Fay's prediction would have been correct, and the Green Knight would have taken off his head.

Q: Explain why the Green Knight did not punish Gawain even though he did not reveal the green lace.

A: The Green Knight understood that Gawain took the lace to save his life and not for the love of another man's wife.

Q: List two of Gawain's most important characteristics.

A: He was both brave and chivalrous. He accepted the challenge of the Green Knight to cut off his head and resisted the temptations of the lady of the castle.

EXPERT COMMENTARY

The anonymous poet who composed *Sir Gawain and the Green Knight* filled his poem with suspense, but the reader is left wondering about the meaning of the 'greenness' of the knight.

> Although the action of the work is relatively simple and straightforward, the events are skillfully arranged and linked. Mysteries abound, concerning for example, the identity and role of an old woman Gawain meets at Bercilak's castle, the identity of the Green Knight himself, and the purpose of the contest. Such questions accumulate and effectively create suspense, but they are eventually answered: the old woman is Morgan Le Fay; the Green Knight and Bercilak are one and the same; and Morgan's purpose in arranging the entire adventure was to test the Round Table and frighten Guinevere.[4]

In his introduction to *Sir Gawain and the Green Knight*, Burton Raffel, translator and scholar, says that the Green Knight has many different human qualities:

> The green knight can be courtly, chivalric, dignified; he can also be rude, boastful, and exceedingly melodramatic. He partakes in short, of the delicate, deliberate ambiguity of the whole poem. He is partly human, partly force of nature; he is partly moral, partly amoral.
>
> . . . Like Gawain, he can speak with dignity and with Right on his side; but also like Gawain, he can seem, whether as green man or as host, considerably less than an ideal symbol of Truth and Goodness. Indeed, those moralizing capital letters seem distinctly out of place anywhere in this poem; it and its poet are far too subtle, too human in the most civilized sense, to indulge in such lack of balance.[5]

5

PERCIVAL

INTRODUCTION

A character named Percival first appeared in Arthurian legends in the late twelfth century. He was an invention of the French romance writer, Chrétien de Troyes (1160–1180), who composed a long story about a courageous young knight who joined Arthur's Round Table. De Troyes's stories were believed to have been commissioned by Marie de Champagne, daughter of Queen Eleanor of Aquitaine (1122–1204). He was the first writer to mention the Grail, Camelot, and Lancelot. His Percival story was supposed to include a spiritual quest that culminated in the young knight seeing the Holy Grail. However, de Troyes ended the story after Percival witnessed a procession in which a young woman carried a golden tray. Percival did not understand the meaning of the procession and did not ask any questions. Other romance writers, however, added continuations to de Troyes's story, and the golden platter became a golden cup: the symbol of the Holy Grail.[1]

Percival was raised by his mother in a small hut at the foot of Mount Snowdon in Wales. Percival's mother did not want her son to know that his dead father and brothers had all been knights and that they had been killed in battle. She feared that if Percival knew that knighthood was his birthright, he would seek it at King Arthur's court and she would lose him just as she had lost his father and brothers.

Percival's mother taught her son that God and the angels were beautiful and that the devil was evil. When Percival was fifteen years old and out hunting in the forest, he came upon a figure riding on a horse. The figure was covered with shining steel armor and Percival believed it to be God. The young boy got down on the ground and offered prayers. After he got up, five similar figures on horses appeared and Percival was sure they must be the angels of God. Again, he got down on the ground and prayed.[2]

The figure on the first horse dismounted and took off his

helmet. He smiled at the naive young man and announced, "I am a knight of King Arthur." The knight explained to Percival that he was not God and that the other knights were not angels. In the end, he told young Percival that if he wanted to be a knight, he should go to Carlisle where Arthur was currently holding court and ask to become a squire.

Percival's mother fainted when she learned that her son had met King Arthur's knights. Then she told her son the truth about his dead father and brothers, but she still would not reveal his father's name. She begged Percival not to seek knighthood, but she could not dissuade him. Her parting advice to her young son was that he must always honor women and that it would be permissible to take from a woman a kiss, if it had been freely offered, a ring, or a small gift, but nothing more. She further advised her son that he must ask gentlemen their names as soon as they met, converse with them, and take their advice. Lastly, she advised him to pray in every church or chapel he came upon.

PERCIVAL

Percival took a deep breath, threw back his shoulders in the manner of a would-be knight, and kissed his mother goodbye. His distraught mother slumped onto the ground and sobbed as her last son rode away.

Percival walked and ran across fresh green valleys and through thick dark forests. He stopped only long enough to ask for directions to the court of King Arthur. Then, after an exhausting week of travel young, Percival came upon a tent beside a stream. Believing the tent was a chapel, Percival stepped quietly inside. There was no altar as his mother had described in his childhood stories, but there was a beautiful young woman asleep on a thick bed of soft blankets. Misconstruing his mother's advice, Percival strode over to the woman and kissed her freely on the lips. While he was kissing her, he noticed a sparkling green ring on one finger and he believed that it was meant for him, so he gently removed it. The young woman was so paralyzed with fear that she was unable to scream. Percival smiled, nodded politely, and left the tent.

That evening when the young woman's lover, the Haughty Knight of the Heath, returned home, she told him about the bold intruder who had kissed her and stolen her ring. The angry lover stormed out of the tent and went in pursuit of the perpetrator.

Young Percival continued his journey, pleased with the ring that would remind him of the beautiful sleeping woman and happy that he was part of a fresh new world.

During the second week of his journey, Percival entered a

clearing and saw far off in the distance a huge stone castle set high on a hill. Percival knew that he had found Camelot just as it had been described to him by the knights in the forest.

Young Percival bowed briefly to the squire at the gate and whisked past him and into the courtyard. There was a great deal of commotion going on inside the castle so Percival hung back by the door. Suddenly, a bold stranger covered in bright red armor bolted out the door passed Percival carrying King Arthur's drinking cup. As the Knights of the Round Table argued over which one of them would pursue the thief, King Arthur raised his arms in the air to gain silence. "It is only a cup," said the king. "I shall not sacrifice one of my knights for a mere cup."

Upon hearing this, young Percival darted into the room. "Please, Sire," he begged, "let me rescue your cup."

King Arthur looked at the sturdy young man in the thick leather tunic and wrinkled his brow. "Are you prepared to die?" he asked.

"Oh, I shall not die," replied Percival. "I shall return very soon with your cup, wearing bright red armor."

The king chuckled and nodded his approval. "Go, my lad."

Percival jumped up on the black stallion that the young squire had readied for him and left Camelot excited to be questing for the king's cup. Percival had guilelessly fallen in love with the bright red armor worn by the thief and wanted it even more than he wanted to rescue the stolen cup. But he intended to recover both.

The sun had begun to disappear below the trees before Percival caught sight of the Red Knight. "Stop," he yelled. "Stop. Now."

The Red Knight turned around and smirked at the wild little boy wearing a leather tunic who charged at him.

"I shall only stop you," replied the Red Knight and he readied his long red lance to unseat the bold young man who rode toward him.

Percival tried to dodge the Red Knight's long, red lance, but it grazed his side and he nearly fell off his horse. Suddenly Percival felt like one of the squirrels he had pursued with his javelin in the forests of Wales. He quickly reached into his belt and pulled out his sharply pointed javelin. With the skill and precision of a primitive hunter, he raised the javelin into the air, took aim, and struck the Red Knight in the neck through a small opening between his helmet and body armor. Fatally wounded, the Red Knight fell to the ground.

After Percival had dismounted, he darted toward the king's cup and scooped it up. After he had set the cup against a tree, Percival set about removing the dead knight's beautiful red armor. He gently stroked each piece of the armor as he removed it from the knight's limp body. But Percival turned his nose up at the feminine-looking red silk tunic that the knight wore beneath his armor. "Oh my," he muttered, "the poor man did not own a sturdy leather tunic such as mine."

Percival wasted no time outfitting himself in the bright red armor before he picked up the king's cup and rode off toward Camelot. Along the way, Percival came upon the castle of a wise baron. Quite mysteriously, the baron knew that the young man disguised as a knight in red armor was really a very naive young man. The wise baron invited Percival to stay with him at his castle. He instructed young Percival on the ways of chivalry and knightly behavior, and advised him to remain silent in the presence of strangers.

After Percival had learned all the baron had to teach him, he bade him goodbye and rode away. Shortly thereafter, he came upon a castle that was under siege by two bold knights. Percival saw and heard a beautiful young maiden calling for help from the castle tower. Putting his chivalry to the test, Percival charged at the knights and drove them away.

"My name is Blanchefleur," called the young woman from the tower. "I shall forever be in your debt. And I pledge my love to you forever."

Pleased at having saved the young woman from harm, Percival rode away smiling.

Many uneventful days passed before Percival came upon the castle of the Fisher King, an old knight so wounded in battle that he spent his days fishing. Upon meeting Percival, the Fisher King invited the young traveler to come inside to warm himself. The rooms of the Fisher King's castle held a warmth and friendliness that reminded young Percival of the small hut that he had lived in with his mother, and he was happy to stay for a while. After the Fisher King excused himself and left the room, Percival sat down on the floor and rested his back against the fireplace wall. While he waited, he closed his eyes. But no sooner had his eyelids fallen shut when he heard the sound of soft, melodic voices. He opened his eyes and saw a long procession passing in front of him. There was a young man carrying a bleeding lance followed by a line of youths carrying candelabra, and at the end, a young woman bearing a golden platter. Obeying the baron's advice to remain silent, Percival said not a word.

Percival fell into a deep sleep and did not awaken until the following morning. He searched for the Fisher King to tell him what had happened and to ask its meaning, but the castle was empty. So Percival rode away, still pondering his experience from the previous night.

Later that day, Percival met a young damsel sobbing by the side of the road. He stopped and asked her why she cried. "My husband has been slain by an angry knight," replied the young woman.

Percival dismounted and walked toward her. "I was going home to visit my mother after I left the Fisher King's castle," said Percival, "but now I will find the villain who murdered your husband before going home." The young woman stopped crying long enough to ask Percival his name and the whereabouts of his mother. "Oh, my," she said. "I am your cousin. And your mother, my aunt, died several months ago."

Percival's body stiffened and tears filled his eyes. "What happened?" he asked.

"They say she died of a broken heart."

Percival leaned his head against the warm body of his patient horse and wept. His cousin waited an appropriate amount of time before speaking. "I am sorry," she said. "But please, tell me what happened at the castle of the Fisher King."

Percival's cousin learned that he had seen the Grail procession but had not asked questions. She admonished him for his stupidity. But Percival had never heard of the Holy Grail.

"The Holy Grail," she explained in a soft voice, "is the cup that Christ drank from during the Last Supper. After He was crucified, Joseph of Arimathea collected His blood in the cup and brought it to Britain from Jerusalem. The cup has been lost for a very long time and can only be found by a pure man free of sin who asks the right questions when he sees the Grail."

"What questions should I have asked?" Percival asked her.

"You should have asked, 'What is the Grail? Whom does it serve?'"

Percival admitted that he had not spoken because he had been warned by the kind baron to remain silent in the presence of strangers.

The young woman said, "Long ago, a battle between two competing kings caused the land to become barren and one of the kings to become wounded. The land cannot be restored and the king cannot be healed until someone asks the meaning of the Grail."

Percival hung his head in shame. "I did not know," he said. Then, he thanked his cousin and said goodbye. Days later, he found the man who had murdered his cousin's husband, defeated him, and ordered him to go to Camelot and report to the king. "Tell King Arthur and the Knights of the Round Table that I have seen the Grail," commanded Percival.

The news that Percival had sighted the Holy Grail created a questing fever among the Knights of the Round Table. By the time Percival returned to Camelot, the Knights of the Round Table had begun to set out in small groups in search of the Grail. However, Percival could not remember how he had come upon the castle of the Fisher King and could not direct them in which direction they should go.

QUESTIONS AND ANSWERS

Q: *Explain the reason why Percival's mother kept his birthright a secret.*

A: Percival's father and brothers had been knights and had all been killed in battle. His mother did not want to lose her last son, so she kept his birthright a secret.

Q: *Describe what happened at Camelot before Percival arrived.*

A: A stranger had come to court and had stolen King Arthur's drinking cup. Arthur's knights argued over who would rescue the cup, but the king did not believe his cup was worthy of a duel. Percival volunteered to rescue the cup. The king warned him of the danger but allowed him to go.

Q: *Why was Percival so eager to risk his life for the king's cup?*

A: He wanted the bright red armor worn by the thief, and the cup was an excuse to go after the knight's armor.

Q: *Describe Percival's first adventure after he outfitted himself in bright red armor.*

A: He visited a castle owned by a knowledgeable baron. The baron invited Percival to stay with him and he taught the young man everything he had to know to become a chivalrous knight.

Q: *Explain the meaning of the Holy Grail.*

A: The Holy Grail was thought to be the cup that Christ drank from during the Last Supper. After Christ had been crucified, Joseph of Arimathea had collected the Lord's blood in the cup and brought it to Britain from Jerusalem. The cup had been lost for a long time and could only be found by a pure man who was free of sin.

6

LANCELOT AND GUINEVERE

INTRODUCTION

An unknown author in A.D. 1220 created five distinct but interrelated Arthurian legends that were called *The Vulgate Cycle*. These stories popularized a young, worldly knight named Lancelot, whom Chrétien de Troyes had created some fifty years earlier. *The Vulgate Cycle* formed the basis of Malory's *Le Morte d'Arthur*, which was written 250 years later.[1]

During the fifth century, hordes of barbarians swept across western Europe and burned and looted towns along the way. In Benwick, France, Lancelot's father, King Ban, dropped dead of a heart attack before he could get his family to safety. His wife, Queen Elaine, was so upset by her husband's sudden death that she did not see the fairy Viviane (The Lady of the Lake) scoop up her young son and take him away while she tended to her husband.

The Lady of the Lake took the baby boy to her fairytale city in the middle of a magical lake called *Bois en Val* (Wooded Valley). She raised him like a son and gave him a first-class knightly education. When Lancelot reached the age of eighteen, the Lady of the Lake outfitted him in white and silver armor, and gave him a fine new sword and a large white shield. Then, she took him to England and presented him to King Arthur's court.[2]

Lancelot soon became the most skillful and best-known of King Arthur's knights. He also became the king and queen's closest friend, and eventually, Queen Guinevere's secret lover.

LANCELOT AND GUINEVERE

Lancelot looked very knightly the day he rode into Camelot alongside the Lady of the Lake. He wore his new white armor and carried his shiny silver shield. The Lady of the Lake rode proudly up to the gate at Camelot as if she were escorting a would-be king.

"I have come to meet with King Arthur," said the Lady of the Lake to the young squire at the gate. The young man smiled and beckoned them to follow him.

Lancelot had never been so happy. He had trained hard and long to become a knight and he could not believe that he had finally arrived at Camelot. "Wait here," said the squire. "I will tell the king you have arrived."

The squire returned and motioned for the visitors to follow him to the king's study. Lancelot and the Lady of the Lake entered the room and bowed politely to the king, who sat in a large ornate chair facing the door. "Welcome to Camelot," said Arthur.

Gripping Lancelot's hand, the Lady of the Lake took a small step forward. "May I introduce my nephew, Lancelot? He is well trained and prepared to assume knighthood."

The king smiled approvingly and explained to the Lady of the Lake the procedure for attaining knighthood. "It is traditional at Camelot for young men to start by serving the queen as a squire," said Arthur. "When the time is right, your nephew will go questing and prove that he is worthy to join the Knights of the Round Table. In the meantime, we will take good care of him."

The Lady of the Lake smiled warmly at the king, gave a small bow, and still gripping Lancelot's hand, they backed out of the room. Lancelot was so excited at having met the king that he squeezed the Lady of the Lake's hand so hard that she winced. "I am sorry," he said. "But I am so happy to be here." Lancelot brushed his blond, curly hair away from his face, gave the Lady of the Lake a small kiss on the cheek, and whispered, "Thank you, dear Aunt. I will make you proud."

Lancelot served the queen as a squire, but he idolized the king and spent all his free time at Arthur's side. The king enjoyed Lancelot's engaging wit and keen intellect and did not object to having the young man around. King Arthur and Lancelot became such good friends that when the king had to attend to business elsewhere in England, he put Lancelot in charge of Camelot.

Lancelot enjoyed life at Camelot, but he was anxious to become a Knight of the Round Table. He asked the king and queen to allow him to go questing. The royal couple understood Lancelot's ambitions, but they wanted his company at home. Finally, the king and queen could not keep him at Camelot any longer and they sent him off with their blessings.

Lancelot traveled far and wide and participated in many dueling and jousting tournaments. The accomplished young man never lost a contest and soon became a legend throughout the land. When Lancelot returned to Camelot, his reputation had already preceded him and King Arthur was eager to include him as a Knight of the Round Table.

After Lancelot was knighted, his friendship with Guinevere slowly blossomed into love and the two could barely stay away from each other. Lancelot, who loved King Arthur as much as he loved the queen, tried very hard to deny his feelings for Guinevere. But the queen wanted him at her side day and night and she showed much less restraint.

Soon, Lancelot became so filled with guilt over their illicit

affair that he began to schedule questing trips that kept him away from Camelot and the queen for long periods of time. When her lover was away, the queen would be sullen and sulk about the court. But when Lancelot returned home, the queen would be lighthearted and carefree. Guinevere's personality changes became obvious to the Knights of the Round Table, but King Arthur, who loved the queen and Lancelot equally, refused to acknowledge the affair and dismissed the rumors that he heard.

One day, the king asked Lancelot if he would visit King Pelles in Corbin and try to determine if Pelles knew where to locate the Holy Grail. "Pelles has the reputation of a madman," said Arthur. "But I would like to know if there is any truth to the rumor."

Always eager to serve the king, Lancelot journeyed to Corbin to meet with King Pelles. Before Lancelot reached the king's castle, however, he was greeted by the people of Corbin, who believed he had come to rescue the king's daughter. Lancelot could not understand what the people were talking about until an old lady stepped out of the crowd and tried to explain. "The daughter of our king is locked in a tower on the hill," said the old lady. "By some form of magic, she has been made to sit in a bath of scalding water for five years."

A low moan wafted over the crowd. "Only the best knight in the world can rescue our young princess," continued the old lady. "And we know that you are that knight."

Lancelot did not believe himself to be the best knight in the world, so he humbly turned his horse around to go home. "No. No. You must not leave," cried a young woman as she stepped in front of Lancelot and blocked his path.

Lancelot dismounted and followed the townspeople up the hill toward the tower. "Morgan Le Fay, the sorceress, did this," said an old man who walked beside Lancelot. "She was jealous of the princess' beauty. Morgan worked her magic to keep the princess locked in the tower so that no one would be able to see her."

Lancelot walked slowly up to the wooden tower door and pushed it open. A red-hot furnace that extended all the way up to the ceiling filled the first floor, and there was a steep narrow staircase at one end of the room. Lancelot climbed the stairs to the top. Thick, hot steam rushed out to meet him when he opened the door at the top of the stairs. Like a blind man, Lancelot stretched his arms out in front of him and walked toward a weak voice that came from the far side of the room. After a few minutes, he could see the outline of a small, young girl sitting bashfully in a tub filled with scalding water. Her skin was bright red all over.

The young girl, knowing that Morgan's magic had to be undone in the proper manner, whispered to Lancelot, "You must give me your hand." She took his hand and led him out of the room, down the stairs, and outside to her loyal friends. The old woman with the gray shawl quickly removed it and wrapped it around the young princess.

Soon, King Pelles came down from his castle to find out what was causing all the commotion. He greeted Lancelot with good cheer and thanked him for having rescued his daughter, Elaine. "Come." said the king. "We shall celebrate."

Lancelot stayed for many weeks at the castle but seldom saw King Pelles and never learned whether he was a madman. But Lancelot did become friendly with the king's butler and they spent many evenings together sampling the king's wines. The butler had tried repeatedly to get Lancelot to spend time with Elaine but Lancelot was not interested. One night, the butler got Lancelot very drunk and arranged for him to receive a message. The young knight read the message, and said, "I must leave immediately—the queen wants to see me."

Without protesting, the butler bade goodbye to Lancelot and the lovesick knight rode off. Lancelot soon found the inn where the queen was waiting, and he spent the night in her arms. But the next morning when Lancelot awoke, he discovered that he had not been with Guinevere—but with the young princess Elaine! Lancelot was furious at having been deceived and spat bitter words at the frightened young girl, who sat there and wept. He accused her of the plotting to make Guinevere jealous. Elaine tried to explain that the evening had been arranged by Morgan Le Fay. "I meant no harm," she pleaded. "I have fallen in love with you."

Lancelot was not interested in Elaine's declaration of love and he became angrier than he had ever been before. He stormed out of the room, leaving the young princess sobbing. He returned to Camelot but kept the incident with Elaine a secret. Lancelot and Queen Guinevere spent many happy hours together making up for the time that Lancelot had been away, but the tranquility at Camelot did not last very long. The following year, a messenger came and announced the arrival of Elaine and Lancelot's son, Galahad. Lancelot had not known about the boy and was embarrassed by Elaine's impudence. The queen would not believe that he had been tricked into staying all night with Elaine. Instead, Guinevere accused him of being unfaithful and they had a terrible fight.

Lancelot could not bear the queen's wrath and, in the midst of the argument, he ran to the window and threw himself out. Guinevere sent a dozen knights to search for Lancelot but he had disappeared. Not long thereafter, Elaine and Galahad returned to their castle at Corbin.

Like a madman, Lancelot wandered from town to town for several years. People took pity on him and gave him food. No one realized that he had been one of King Arthur's bravest and most noble of knights. Lancelot had lost most of his body weight. He was unshaven, delirious, and dirty when Elaine finally found him near Corbin. Having sent their son Galahad to a nunnery to be educated, Elaine was all alone and more than willing to nurse the man she loved back to health. Although Lancelot knew that he did not deserve her love and kindness, he stayed with Elaine for several years.

One day when Lancelot was healthy enough to go hunting, he met his cousin, Sir Bors, in the forest. "Lancelot! Lancelot!" exclaimed Bors. "Where have you been? Queen Guinevere has had men searching for you for many years."

The mere mention of Guinevere's name caused all the old desires to rise up in Lancelot's veins and he suddenly ached to return to Camelot. He explained to Bors that Elaine had saved his life and that he could not leave her.

"Am I to understand that you do not love Guinevere?" asked Bors.

Lancelot hung his head. Although Bors and everyone at Camelot knew that he loved Guinevere, no man had said it aloud. Lancelot could not bear the pain of his old desires and he did not want to think about Guinevere, so he turned and rode away without speaking.

Lancelot brooded for several weeks and Elaine feared the worst. Elaine had always known that Lancelot did not love her, but she did not care because she loved him enough for both of them. They went through the motions of living together for many more months, but Lancelot's mind and heart had already returned to his beloved Guinevere.

Finally, Lancelot could stay away no longer. "Elaine," he whispered. "I must return to Camelot."

Elaine pleaded with him to stay and reminded him that she had saved his life after he had gone mad. "You shall go mad again if you return," cried Elaine. "Guinevere can never be yours. Can't you understand that?" But Lancelot could not be dissuaded, and after a tearful departure, Lancelot rode away. Elaine knew that she would never see him again.

Fifteen happy years passed at Camelot, and no mention was made of Elaine or Galahad. Then, one day a handsome young man with curly, blonde hair and flashing blue eyes rode into Camelot and asked to be made a Knight of the Round Table.

King Arthur was immediately reminded of Lancelot, who had come to Camelot with the Lady of the Lake many years before. Tears filled the king's weary eyes as he stretched out his hands to the handsome youth. "Welcome, Galahad," he said. "We will take good care of you at Camelot."

QUESTIONS AND ANSWERS

Q: *What were the circumstances that led to Lancelot's upbringing?*

A: Although Lancelot, the son of King Bans, was born in Benwick, France, his family had to flee from their homeland after barbarian invaders burned their village. While his mother tended to his dying father, Lancelot was taken by the Lady of the Lake to a fairytale city called Bois en Val, which was in the middle of a magical lake.

Q: *How did Lancelot become a Knight at King Arthur's Round Table?*

A: The Lady of the Lake gave Lancelot a first-class knightly education and took him to England. She presented him to King Arthur when he was eighteen years old.

Q: *Explain the circumstances that led to the friendship and subsequent love affair between Lancelot and the queen.*

A: Before Lancelot became a knight, he served as one of the queen's squires. He and the king became good friends and King Arthur eventually left business at Camelot in Lancelot's hands when he traveled. Lancelot spent most of his time with the queen and their friendship eventually blossomed into love.

Q: *Describe King Pelles' reputation.*

A: King Pelles, who lived in Corbin, was said to have knowledge of the Holy Grail. However, Pelles also had the reputation of being a madman. Arthur sent Lancelot to Corbin to see if the rumors were true.

Q: *Describe Lancelot's experience in Corbin.*

A: Lancelot was met by the people of the town who begged him to rescue King Pelles' daughter, Princess Elaine. She had been sitting in a bath of scalding water for five years.

Q: Who was responsible for having locked the princess in the tower? And why was it done?

A: Morgan Le Fay's sorcery kept the princess sitting in a bath of scalding water because she was jealous of the princess' beauty and did not want others to see her.

Q: Explain how Morgan Le Fay plotted to deceive Lancelot.

A: Morgan sent a note that seemed to have come from Queen Guinevere, asking Lancelot to meet her at a nearby inn. Lancelot spent the night at the inn, not with Queen Guinevere, but with Princess Elaine. Morgan Le Fay had worked her sorcery and put Elaine in the queen's place.

Q: List two of Queen Guinevere's most obvious characteristics.

A: She was jealous and self-centered. She scolded Lancelot for his relationship with Elaine and refused to give up her adulterous affair with Lancelot.

Q: Describe the queen's reaction to Elaine's visit and the knowledge of Lancelot's infidelity.

A: Guinevere was furious. She argued with Lancelot and refused to believe that Morgan Le Fay's magic had arranged for their stay at the Inn. Her raging caused Lancelot to jump out of a castle window.

EXPERT COMMENTARY

Lancelot is one of the most famous Knights of the Round Table. Here, scholars Lacy and Ashe describe the characteristic most often associated with the young knight.

> Lancelot's best-known role is as the illicit lover of Guinevere. The Queen is high-handed and callous toward him, as the conventions of courtly love require, but their liaison, however tempestuous at times, is deep-rooted and enduring. It is intertwined with the Grail theme.
>
> . . . Lancelot does not achieve the Grail himself, because of his adulterous love, yet ironically the same sin has produced Galahad, the knight who does.[3]

The sin of Lancelot and Guinevere pervaded King Arthur's court, but Richard Barber in *The Arthurian Legends* suggests that Arthur shared the blame:

> It is in his match with Guinevere that Arthur fails. He misjudges Lancelot, misjudges Guinevere, failing to see the other side of the coin, the carnal passions which move him not at all. He chooses Guinevere partly because only the beautiful bride can match his position and spiritual attainment, forgetting that earthly and heavenly beauty are not one and the same thing.[4]

7

GALAHAD

INTRODUCTION

Sir Galahad was first mentioned in *The Vulgate Cycle*, a group of Arthurian legends composed by an unknown author in A.D. 1220. Later, in A.D. 1470, Sir Thomas Malory made Galahad a fully developed character who accomplished a whole series of miracles during his quest for the Holy Grail.

Galahad was the son of Sir Lancelot and Princess Elaine of Corbin. His parents never married, and young Galahad grew up not knowing his father. He spent his childhood with his mother and grandfather, King Pelles, in their Corbin castle. When it was time for Galahad to be formally educated, his grandfather took him to a reputable nunnery where the little boy received an excellent education. When Galahad turned eighteen years of age, King Pelles sent a messenger to Camelot and requested that Lancelot come to the nunnery. Lancelot had not seen Galahad since Elaine brought him to Camelot shortly after he was born. and the now-famous knight was eager to claim him.[1]

Until Galahad came to Camelot, Lancelot had been known as the bravest and most noble knight in the land. But Galahad surprised Lancelot and members of the court by taking the *Siege Perilous*, the last empty seat at the Round Table—which was reserved for the purest knight in the world.[2]

GALAHAD

The annual Pentecost celebration was in full swing. King Arthur and the Knights of the Round Table had just finished eating when, suddenly, they heard the clambering of hoofs on the stone floor of the dining hall. A lovely young damsel riding a pure white stallion had entered the room.

"Is Lancelot about?" she asked breathlessly. "King Pelles has requested that he come straight away. For what reason, I know not," said the young damsel.

Lancelot got up from the table and nodded to the young woman on the horse. He understood that King Pelles would not call for him without good reason. "Excuse me," said Lancelot. "I must not keep Pelles waiting." Then, Lancelot and the young damsel rode away.

After they had ridden through the forest for several hours, they came upon a well-protected stone abbey, or monastery, set atop a small hill. A young squire met them at the gate, took their horses, and led them inside. Lancelot followed a small, serious-looking nun, who led him into a large room furnished with one spare wooden bench. "Please be seated, Sire," said the nun. And she walked hastily out of the room.

Minutes later, several nuns escorted a handsome, golden-haired youth into the room. The nuns recognized the young man's likeness to Lancelot and smiled warmly. Although Lancelot's honey-toned hair had turned white, his full, broad smile and glistening blue eyes matched those of the young man who stood before him. "Sire," said one of the nuns, "we have taken care to raise Galahad to be a worthy and noble gentleman. He is prepared to become a knight."

Lancelot was very proud. He wanted to step forward and hug his son, but he restrained himself. Lancelot smiled and touched Galahad on the arm. "We will go to chapel in the morning," said Lancelot, "and before we return to Camelot, you will be a knight."

The following morning before they began their journey, Lancelot kept his promise and knighted his young son. Then, father and son thanked the nuns and bade them goodbye.

When Galahad and his father arrived at Camelot, they found that King Arthur and the Knights of the Round Table had gone down to the river. Lancelot left Galahad in the castle and went to join his friends who stood staring at a huge chunk of red marble with a sword in it that floated on the water. The inscription on the stone indicated that the sword was meant for the best knight in all the world.

King Arthur was excited when Lancelot arrived, because the king believed that the sword was meant for his good friend. "Remove the sword from the stone," commanded Arthur, reaching out to take Lancelot's hand. But Lancelot pulled away. "I cannot try to remove the sword, Sire, for if I fail I shall one day be mortally wounded by it. The sword belongs only to the knight destined to achieve the Holy Grail."

Sir Gawain believed that Lancelot was being just a bit too humble, so he stepped forward and offered to pull the sword out of the stone. Gawain pulled and pulled. But the sword would not budge. Percival, who was more muscular and even stronger than Gawain, stepped forward after Gawain gave up trying. Percival's superior strength, however, did not make the sword budge from its holder.

At last, Arthur suggested that they return to the castle and enjoy their meal. King Arthur and his knights were eating, drinking, and enjoying great laughter when the shutters on the dining hall windows slammed shut and the room became heavy with darkness. As the knights sat silently in the dark, a long beam of white light began to rise from the empty seat reserved for the Siege Perilous. It floated straight upward like a long silver ribbon being pulled into the air. Then, as if the ribbon had been yanked through the ceiling, it disappeared. King Arthur's words were hardly audible: "The Siege Perilous is prepared to be filled."

King Arthur had barely taken his seat when an old man wearing a long white robe entered the hall, followed by a handsome young knight. Lancelot recognized the knight as Galahad, but the old man had appeared out of nowhere.

"I have brought this young knight, Galahad, who is of royal lineage," said the old man, "and the most pure of heart." Galahad wore no armor, did not carry a shield, and an empty scabbard hung from his side.

After Arthur welcomed the strangers, the old man lead Galahad to the Siege Perilous. The Knights of the Round Table held their breath as Galahad sat down. But the seat did not burst into flames the way it had when others had sat in it. Everyone in the room marveled that the young man could sit so securely in a seat that had been empty for a generation. Then, Galahad's name mysteriously appeared in gold and black letters on the back of the seat.

In an effort to return to the reality of the day, Arthur stood up and announced, "Sir Galahad's scabbard is empty. We must take him down to the river." The Knights of the Round Table got up and followed the king to the river. When Galahad saw the sword embedded in the red marble floating in the water, he smiled like a child who had just found his lost ball. Then, with the grace of a mature man and the steadiness of a soldier, the fresh young knight reached out toward the sword and gently drew it out of the red marble. King Arthur and his knights gave a loud cheer.

But no sooner had the knights turned back toward the castle when a young damsel came riding toward them. "Nucien, the hermit, has announced that the Holy Grail shall appear in his house," she cried. "Go there tomorrow."

Arthur had dreaded the day when his knights would

finally quest for the Grail. He knew that they would leave Camelot and not return until they had found it—if one of them ever did. In an effort to assume cheerfulness, the king requested that his knights hold one last jousting tournament before they left on their quest. "Today, we shall play for the last time," said the king. "And tonight we shall celebrate."

Galahad was given a white shield decorated with a red cross that was believed to have been drawn using the blood of Joseph of Arimathea. He wore a suit of armor, a helmet, and carried his newly acquired sword in his scabbard. Galahad rode confidently among the knights for several hours and unseated all challengers except Lancelot and Percival, who remained superior horsemen.

That evening before dinner had been served, Arthur raised his wine goblet and made a toast to Galahad: "To the purest knight in all the land."

The festivities were in full swing when the wind began to blow and great claps of thunder sounded over the castle. A sudden gust of wind blew in through an open window and extinguished the dining hall's candles. When the wind subsided, a shining light filled the room with eerie brightness. Then, an object covered by a pure white cloth woven with threads of gold floated within the light beam. It hung in the center of the light for a few seconds before it slipped back up the light shaft and disappeared.

Percival recognized the event as the same one he had witnessed in the castle of the Fisher King. His cousin had described its appearance as that of the Holy Grail.

At last, Gawain rose and declared that the assembly had been given the sign to begin questing for the Grail. "Tomorrow, I shall leave to seek the Grail," said Gawain, "and I vow I shall not return to Camelot until I have seen it."

After Gawain raised his cup, Galahad stood and repeated the vow. Then, all the Knights of the Round Table raised their cups and vowed as one.

QUESTIONS AND ANSWERS

Q: *Who were Galahad's parents?*

A: Galahad's mother was Princess Elaine of Corbin and Sir Lancelot of Camelot. The couple never married and only lived together during the time when Lancelot was recuperating from his mad wanderings.

Q: *Explain why the Knights of the Round Table were down at the river when Lancelot and Galahad arrived at Camelot.*

A: A sword embedded in a large red marble stone had been found floating in the river. The sword could only be removed by the best knight in the whole world.

Q: *Describe the efforts made to remove the sword from the red marble.*

A: Lancelot rejected the king's request to remove the sword because he believed that if he failed, he would be wounded by it one day. After Percival and Gawain tried and failed, the king and the Knights of the Round table returned to the castle.

Q: *What was the significance of the Siege Perilous?*

A: It was the seat reserved for the purist knight in the world and it would go up in flames if taken by any other person.

Q: *Describe the sign given to the Knights of the Round Table that made them vow to quest for the Holy Grail.*

A: A strong beam of light shone in through an open window of the dining hall and carried within it an object covered by a pure white cloth woven with threads of gold. The object was believed to have been the Grail cup.

EXPERT COMMENTARY

In A.D. 1200, an unknown French author wrote a compressed version of a young knight's early adventures including his quest of the Grail. The knight was presumed to have been Galahad, although he was not mentioned by name until publication of *The Vulgate Cycle* twenty years later. Scholars Lacy and Ashe believe these stories created a lifelike image of Galahad:

> He is handsome, and skillful in combat, but his chief quality is chastity, which is here made vital for the full experience of the Grail—one consequence being that Lancelot, despite his noble qualities, is doomed to fail in the Quest and succeed only by proxy through his son.[3]

The scholar Roger Sherman Loomis claims that investigation into the names of the ancestors of the Grail hero Galahad indicates that he was of Celtic origin:

> The most extended account of the early history of the Grail, its origin as a relic which had touched the lips and held the blood of the Savior of the World, its acquisition by Joseph of Aramathea, its transportation to Britain, and the many marvels and miracles which attended those who cared for it until the time of Arthur, is in the first part of the *Vulgate Cycle*. . . It contains the names and the stories of the ancestors of the Grail hero, who in this cycle is Galaad. . . He is distinguished by his precocious youth, his gift of prophecy, his knowledge of the stars, and his occasional solitary sojourns in the forest.[4]

8

MORDRED

INTRODUCTION

Arthur was still a young bachelor king when he met Morgause at Camelot shortly after his coronation. He was aware that Morgause was married to King Lot of Orkney, but he did not know that she was his half-sister. That evening, Morgause seduced Arthur and, as a result, Mordred was conceived.

That same night, Arthur had a dream in which a serpent came out of his side and destroyed him, his land, and his people. It was such a horrible dream that Arthur had it rendered in a painting that he kept in his castle in the hope that one day he would come to understand its meaning.[1]

Soon thereafter, Merlyn told Arthur that Morgause was his half-sister and that she would bear a son on May Day. When the young king learned that his father, King Pendragon, was also Morgause's father, he felt deceived and shamed. For the first time ever, Arthur became angry with his friend and mentor Merlyn. "Why didn't you tell me this?" asked Arthur.

Merlyn hung his head in shame. "I did not think it would be necessary just yet. Morgause is older than you are and married. How was I to know that you would end up together?" Then Merlyn advised Arthur that the only way to hide his incestuous relationship with Morgause would be to have all baby boys born to noblemen on May Day sent out to sea in leaky boats. Merlyn prophesied that if Arthur's son was allowed to live he would eventually destroy the king.[2]

Merlyn's plan was distasteful to Arthur. The wizard had to convince the young king that he must carry out the plan for the good of the kingdom.

Quite miraculously, all the babies that had been sent out to sea drowned except for Mordred, who washed up onto the shore of a small Orkney island off the coast of present-day Scotland. He was rescued by a fisherman and his wife, who suspected that the little boy they nurtured was of noble birth. Still, they kept him and raised him until he was fourteen years old. Then, they took him to Camelot.[3]

MORDRED

After Mordred was knighted at Camelot, he was made welcome by the knights of the Round Table. Everyone at Camelot believed that Mordred was the youngest son of King Lot and Queen Morgause, Arthur's half-sister. Only the royal couple's four sons (Gawain, Agravaine, Gaheris, and Gareth, who were already Knights of the Round Table), knew that Mordred was only a half-brother. But they kept the family's secret. Mordred was pleased to discover that his parents were the king and queen of Orkney.

During his first two years at King Arthur's court, Mordred became friends with Lancelot and showed great promise as a knight. One day the two friends decided to enter a jousting tournament at Peningue Castle in Surluse and they rode out of Camelot in high spirits. As they rode, Mordred boasted about his skills and Lancelot listened and chuckled. Before reaching Peningue, the knights met an old priest who was kneeling before a large tomb. As they approached, the priest got up off his knees and spoke as if he knew them, "Indeed, you are the two most unfortunate knights I have ever met," said the holy man.

Lancelot and Mordred did not know what the old man was talking about. But the priest did not wait for them to ask questions. Instead, he told Mordred that he was not King Lot's son, but Arthur's. "You will eventually destroy Arthur and do more harm in your lifetime than all of his ancestors have

done good," said the old priest. And as he walked away, he mumbled, "Arthur will soon learn that you are the serpent that appeared in his dream."

Furious at the priest's revelation about his real father and disgusted by the old man's depressing prophecy, Mordred drew his sword from its scabbard and killed the holy man with one stroke. Lancelot was horrified, but he could not punish Mordred because he had been guilty of having killed men for even lesser offenses. Lancelot hung his head in shame for his companion. Secretly, he wished that Mordred had not killed the priest until the old man had predicted his own future.

Lancelot and Mordred returned to Camelot, but Mordred could not let go of his anger. He was furious that Arthur had not welcomed him to Camelot as a son and even angrier that the king had tried to have him drowned. Mordred did not speak about his desire to be an heir to the throne, but all his energy was secretly directed toward schemes that might make it happen.

Because they were already distinguished knights, Mordred's half-brothers took the sullen young man under their wing. Lancelot had grown tired of Mordred's whining and had begun to avoid him. Mordred became less and less popular with all of the knights as he privately mocked the king's concept of goodness and righteousness. When other Knights of the Round Table returned from quests and reported chivalrous deeds, Mordred privately scorned their stupidity.

Before long, Mordred began to speak of nothing but plots to overthrow the king. His brothers tried to make Mordred understand that King Arthur had also been deceived and that their own mother had been equally as guilty. They tried to soothe Mordred's pain but the anger that filled his veins could not be calmed.

One night, after Mordred and Agravaine had drunk too much wine, Mordred suggested that they make a plan and organize an army to overthrow King Arthur. "But how are you to organize people to fight against a king they love? People will not fight just because you have a personal hatred for the man," said Agravaine. "They will need a reason to overthrow their king."

Mordred tried to convince Agravaine that people would join him if they heard his story. But Agravaine argued that it would be too difficult to explain and might not inspire people to go to battle. Agravaine had mixed feelings about helping Mordred. He could not forgive the king for trying to have his own son killed, but Arthur had been a good uncle and Agravaine loved him. Believing that Mordred sought revenge for ill treatment and not that he wanted to be king, Agravaine tried to help his half-brother come up with ideas.

"Suppose you were to expose Queen Guinevere's love affair with Sir Lancelot, the king's most beloved knight? Now that the king has established laws for the country, he would have to try the queen for adultery and Sir Lancelot for treason. And that would destroy the reign of King Arthur."

This idea was only indirectly aimed at the king. Agravaine had long been in love with the queen and was jealous of Lancelot's affair with Guinevere. Agravaine also hated that Lancelot's had such a wonderful reputation as a knight. . . and he knew that a plan that exposed the adulterous couple would also end Lancelot's career.

Agravaine's idea did not excite Mordred because the king had been made aware of his wife's adulterous behavior and had chosen to ignore the affair because he loved the adulterers too much. Agravaine and Mordred discussed the idea for a long time that night and then they both fell asleep.

Several weeks went by, and for lack of a better plan, Mordred began to warm up to Agravaine's idea. Mordred tried out the scheme on Gawain, Gaharis, and Gareth. To his surprise, he discovered that his half-brothers were also so jealous of Lancelot that they would agree to go along with any plot that might destroy the famous knight.

For several weeks, Mordred secretly followed Lancelot from one end of Camelot to the other. He calculated when he would visit the queen and how long he would stay. Then, he devised a plan.

"It will be simple," declared Mordred. "We will hide outside of the queen's bedchamber and after Lancelot is inside, we will knock on the door and demand that they come out. Then we will take the two lovers directly to the king." Mordred was breathless with excitement. "The king will have to try the queen for adultery, and Lancelot will have to be tried for willful violation of allegiance to his country, or treason!"

On the appointed evening, after the king had gone to his study to sign important papers, Mordred and his brothers crept quietly up the long stairway to the queen's bedchamber and hid in the shadows of the hallway outside her door. After the queen's handmaidens had retired for the evening, Lancelot came to her bedchamber and knocked softly on the door. Mordred and his men waited until they were sure that the lovers were trapped inside before they banged on the heavy oak door and demanded that it be opened.

Lancelot had come to the queen's room unarmed and without armor. He knew that Mordred and his men were armed and that he had no means of escape. In a fit of panic, Lancelot opened the door, grabbed the neck of the knight who stood closest to the door, dragged him into the room, and bolted the door behind him. After Lancelot had knocked the young knight unconscious, he grabbed his sword and shield. Without hesitation, he opened the door a second time and went out swinging the sword. Lancelot knocked two knights to the ground before Mordred and the others got away.

Mordred went directly to King Arthur and told him that he had caught Lancelot and the queen together in the queen's own bedchamber and that Lancelot had killed some of his men trying to escape.

Lancelot, however, had not tried to escape. He had rested his exhausted body against a wall leading to the king's study. His shoulders slumped forward and his breath came in shallow spurts as he tried to prepare himself for his admission of guilt. He could not bear the pain that his confession would cause his dear friend. Lancelot loved Arthur almost as much as he loved Guinevere, and he had long dreaded this confrontation.

A squire let Lancelot into the king's study. Arthur sat motionlessly in his chair staring at his old friend. "It has finally come to this," said the king. Lancelot hung his head. He could not make eye contact with Arthur. "For so many years I had hoped this whole affair would go away and that I would not have to punish the two people I love the most," lamented the king. "But you have flaunted your sins. You and Guinevere have made it impossible for me to ignore your adulterous affair."

"Forgive me," whispered Lancelot. "Forgive me for hurting you."

Arthur stood up and walked toward Lancelot. "Guinevere must be tried for adultery," he said sadly, "and you must be tried for treason."

The court at Camelot debated punishment for several weeks. Lancelot's friends at the Round Table presented arguments in his defense but they were unable to convince the jury of his innocence. In the end, the court found Guinevere and Lancelot guilty. The queen's punishment was to be burned alive at the stake. Lancelot was to be banished from Britain.

On the day that the queen was to be executed, men piled firewood around her feet as she stood tied to a stake in the courtyard. Guinevere sobbed hysterically and tugged at the ropes that tied her hands. The king, who had been watching out the window of his study, covered his ears, turned his back to the window, and sunk to the floor sobbing. He could not listen, nor could he watch his beloved queen suffer.

In the courtyard, great crowds gathered around the queen's platform. Many people wept. Others just stood in silence and watched. At midday, the court's highest judge climbed onto a small wooden platform high above the queen.

The judge raised his right arm into the air and the men in the courtyard began to light their torches. Then, the judge raised his left arm into the air and the men set their torches into the firewood that surrounded the queen. Immediately, flames leaped into the air and Queen Guinevere began to scream.

Just as the flames were about to consume the queen, the gates of Camelot flew open and Lancelot and a large group of his supporters burst into the crowd with their swords flashing. Lancelot cut down any man who tried to get between him and the flames that threatened his beloved Guinevere. After he reached the platform, Lancelot untied the queen from the stake, placed her firmly on his horse, and rode out of Camelot.

When the king heard the commotion below, he got up and looked out of the window. A broad smiled crossed his swollen face when he saw the queen and Lancelot make their escape. But Mordred, angrier than he had ever been before, stormed into the castle vowing revenge against Lancelot.

QUESTIONS AND ANSWERS

Q: *Explain the circumstances of Mordred's birth.*

A: Mordred was conceived after Arthur and Morgause spent the night together. Arthur knew that Morgause was married, but he did not know that she was also his half-sister.

Q: *Describe Merlyn's reaction to the birth of Mordred.*

A: Merlyn prophesied that Mordred would destroy the king if he were allowed to live. He suggested that all male babies born on May Day be sent out to sea in leaky boats.

Q: *Explain the importance of Mordred's rescue.*

A: Mordred's rescue by the fisherman made him a potential threat to Arthur's throne if his birthright became known. Mordred, like his father, was born after an illicit affair that could not be revealed.

Q: *Explain the impact of the priest's disclosure on Mordred.*

A: Mordred became so angry that he killed the priest. He was furious with Arthur for not having acknowledged him as a son and for trying to have him killed.

Q: *Describe the plot that Mordred thought of to disgrace the king.*

A: Mordred conspired with his half-brothers to trap Queen Guinevere and Lancelot together, expose their adulterous affair, and take them to King Arthur for punishment.

Q: *What eventually happened to the queen and Lancelot?*

A: The queen was found guilty of adultery and sentenced to be burned alive at the stake. Lancelot's willful violation of allegiance to his country, or treason, had him banished from Britain.

EXPERT COMMENTARY

Arthurian scholar Georges Duby claims that early English literature included many stories that had to do with courtly love and jealousy:

> Not the least of the causes of domestic tension was jealousy. Indeed, in one sense the institution of courtly love was a fantastic elaboration of the theme of jealousy, since the husband, who made love possible, also made it dangerous. In Arthurian literature, however, the king is little affected.
>
> . . .The effects of adulterous love on private life do not begin to appear until the thirteenth century.[4]

The Book of Merlyn was not included in T. H. White's *The Once and Future King*, but appeared much later as a single volume. It was written in 1941 and intended to be an antidote for war. The story includes Arthur's final confrontation with Mordred:

> But a darker fate also dictated his [Arthur's] ignorant siring of an illegitimate son by his own half sister and forced his wife Guencver [Guinevere] and his best knight Lancelot into each other's arms, thus causing rivalry, deceit, and jealousy among the knights.
>
> These last proved to be the old king's downfall. Forgotten were his achievements for the Might of Right and for peace on earth. Forgotten too was his own anguish at having tried his best and failed. The Quest had led nowhere, the Round Table was dispersed. Now Guenever was besieged by Mordred and his Thrashers in the Tower of London and Lancelot was exiled in France, both victims of Mordred's obsession to gain Arthur's throne.[5]

9

THE DEATH OF ARTHUR

INTRODUCTION

During Lancelot's brave rescue of Queen Guinevere when she was about to be burned at the stake, Agravaine and Gareth, Gawain's younger brothers, were killed. Gawain locked himself in the room that he had shared for so many years with his younger brothers and sobbed uncontrollably. When at last he regained his composure, he pleaded with King Arthur to seek revenge on Lancelot.

Mordred did his best to help Gawain round up support for war against Lancelot. He made Arthur believe that he, too, grieved for his half-brothers. Arthur was so upset and confused that he could not decide what to do. He did not want to declare war against his beloved friend, yet his favorite nephew was sick with grief. Arthur's dream for a perfect society had deteriorated into a state of chaos. Never had the knights of the Round Table quested after one of their own, but now Gawain had become so obsessed with his need for revenge that he wanted to kill Lancelot.

Emotions began to run high at court and, eventually, Arthur agreed to send a messenger to France to inform Lancelot that he was declaring war against him. Although many of Lancelot's loyal friends had followed him to France, a considerable number of Arthur's knights remained at Camelot and supported Gawain.

When the time came to leave Camelot, Arthur asked Mordred to stay behind and take care of business at home. The conniving young knight was overjoyed. Mordred squirmed with pleasure as he waved goodbye to Arthur, Gawain, and the army that set out for France. He had long dreamed of becoming king and, unknowingly, Arthur had made that dream come true.[1]

THE DEATH OF ARTHUR

Mordred strutted from the king's study to the royal bedchamber and from the courtyard of Camelot to the king's precious rose garden. Each time he repeated his rounds, he took in more air and his chest grew broader. Mordred's smile was so steady that it seemed he was being tickled from the inside. When he was satisfied that the king and his army had safely landed in France, Mordred set his plan in motion to become the new king of Britain. His first act was to spread word throughout the kingdom that King Arthur had been killed in France during a battle with Lancelot. Then he went through the formalities of setting up a new Parliament. But the best part of his plan was to make Queen Guinevere his wife. Mordred located the nunnery where the queen had been hiding and brought her back to Camelot. When Guinevere returned home, Mordred informed her that he had inherited the throne because Arthur had been killed in France. To convince the Queen that Arthur was dead, Mordred arranged to have forged letters delivered from the battlefield that confirmed the king's death. "You shall become my queen," sneered the evil Mordred. But Queen Guinevere had never been as naïve about Mordred's guile as Arthur had been. She merely gritted her teeth and pretended to go along with his nasty plans.

"First, I must go to London," said the queen. "I cannot marry in the old clothes that I presently own."

Mordred was so sure of the mastery of his plan that he allowed Queen Guinevere to go shopping in London. But the queen had a plan of her own. Upon her arrival in London, she began to purchase enough provisions to last her for many months. Then, she had everything carted to the Tower of London—and she promptly locked herself inside.

Mordred was so furious at having been outwitted that he went to London with a large army and fired cannons at the Tower. But a very powerful old bishop threatened to place the curse of the church on Mordred if he continued his attack. The bishop's threat frightened the cowardly Mordred. He turned his attack upon the bishop, instead.

In the meantime, Arthur's army had laid siege to Lancelot's castle. They fought valiantly for many weeks but each encounter ended in a draw. One day, Lancelot and Gawain came face to face in a field and Lancelot apologized to Gawain for the deaths of his brothers. Lancelot tried to make his friend understand that he had not been aware that Agravaine and Gareth had been Mordred's supporters. He also admitted that he had not recognized them at the gate of Camelot the day he rescued the queen. "Please lay down your sword," begged Lancelot. "I do not want to kill you."

But Gawain was so filled with anger that he lunged at Lancelot and aimed his sword at the opening in his neck armor. Lancelot, however, was a superior swordsman and he expertly dodged the attack. They fought for several hours before Lancelot finally tired of their duel and dealt Gawain a serious wound in the right thigh.

Gawain's wound was so severe that he could not get up. He lay on the ground until Arthur came and took him back to his camp. Arthur tended his nephew with loving kindness but Gawain's leg bled profusely and Arthur could not stop the bleeding. While Arthur tended Gawain, a messenger from England came with the news that Mordred had made himself the new king of England.

Gawain's ghostly white skin suddenly blazed red when he heard the news. He rose slowly up onto one elbow and, using all the strength he could muster, he gasped his last words, "Summon Lancelot for help. Take him to England and defeat Mordred."

Arthur sent the messenger back to England to tell Mordred that he would be returning home and that they should meet on the battlefield. But before the army had completely packed up to leave, Gawain died.

King Arthur agreed to meet Mordred on the Plain of Camlann near the River Camel in Cornwall.[2] Even though Mordred believed that Arthur would surrender, he had advised his men that their swords should be in a ready position at all times. "If a sword is pulled from its scabbard," Mordred advised, "fight!"

Arthur and Mordred arranged their men at opposite ends of a broad open field. While their silent armies waited behind them, father and son walked slowly toward each other.

When the king was within the earshot of Mordred, he said, "I trusted you and I always treated you like a son. You have been most disloyal." Before Mordred could respond, a soldier in the front line of Arthur's command grabbed his sword to stab a small poisonous snake that had dropped out of a tree and onto his shoulder. Mordred and his men, not realizing why the soldier had drawn his sword, drew their swords and began to fight. Arthur and his men did not know what had happened and there was no time to ask questions. Within minutes, the two armies had become engaged in mortal combat. The fighting went on all day and the field became strewn with broken armor and dead bodies. By the time darkness covered the battlefield, hundreds of Arthur's finest knights lay dead. The weary king walked among his men in a daze. The sight of so much needless death slowly turned his grief to anger. He had not seen his son's body among the dead and assumed he was still alive. Arthur began to call out Mordred's name. At last, he found the evil young man still wearing his nasty sneer and leaning wearily against a tree. Arthur drew his sword and charged at Mordred like a wounded boar. Although his heart ached that such feelings had become directed toward his own son, Arthur wanted to kill Mordred. His son, however, was exhausted and could barely defend himself against Arthur's wild fury. They struggled for a long time before Mordred fell to

the ground, mortally wounded. Mordred had also given the old king a fatal wound. Arthur's wound, so typical of everything he had been dealt by his son, was neither swift nor clean. He slumped down against a tree and clutched at his chest. Arthur's breath came in slow, weak spurts.

When Sir Bors found Mordred lying dead and Arthur propped up against a tree gasping for breath, he rushed to the king's side. "Throw Excalibur into the lake," gasped Arthur.

Bors picked up Excalibur and walked to the lake. But he was unable to throw away such a magnificent and magical sword. So, he hid it among the reeds along the shore. When Bors returned to Arthur, he told him that Excalibur was gone. Arthur's sad eyes pleaded with Bors, "You have lied. Excalibur has not been thrown away." Embarrassed, Bors returned to the lake for the second time. But still he could not throw away the royal sword. When he returned the second time, the old man's face was filled with rage. "I cannot die until Excalibur has been thrown into the lake. Now do it!" he exclaimed.

This time Bors returned to the lake, took Excalibur out from among the reeds and threw it far out into the middle of the lake. Excalibur sailed through the air until it was caught by a ghostly white hand. The hand gripped the sword and disappeared beneath the dark blue water.

As Bors turned to walk away, he saw a small boat carrying several beautiful women dressed in flowing black gowns beckoning to him. "We have come for the king," they said. Bors recognized the Lady of the Lake and Morgan Le Fay, Arthur's half-sister. The women stood together on the boat and stretched out their arms toward the king.

"I must join them," whispered Arthur.

Bors lifted the dying king off the ground and they shuffled slowly down toward the water. When the king had been lifted safely aboard the little boat, a soft chorus of mourning voices filled the cool night air. Arthur's devoted knight, Sir Bors, watched as the little boat floated off into the distance. Morgan Le Fay had come to take her dying brother to Avalon, a mystical island far off in the west.

QUESTIONS AND ANSWERS

Q: *Explain why Gawain wanted King Arthur to wage war against Lancelot.*

A: Gawain was grieved by the deaths of his brothers, Agravaine and Gareth, who had been killed at the gates of Camelot the day Lancelot and his men rescued the queen. He wanted to avenge his brothers' deaths.

Q: *Describe Queen Guinevere's reaction to Mordred's claim to the throne.*

A: The queen had never liked her stepson and she could not be fooled by his evil plans. After Mordred had the queen taken from the nunnery where she had been hidden and brought to Camelot to be his wife, she convinced him that she must first go to London and buy new clothes for the wedding. After the queen arrived in London, she locked herself in the Tower of London so that Mordred could not get her.

Q: *Describe Gawain's battle with Lancelot in France.*

A: Both sides fought valiantly for many weeks, but neither side could claim victory. Eventually, Lancelot and Gawain dueled one-on-one, and Lancelot fatally injured Gawain in the right thigh.

Q: *Describe Arthur's reaction to the news that Mordred had made himself king of England.*

A: The king sent a message to Mordred asking to meet him and settle their dispute on the plain of Camlann near the Camel River in Cornwall.

Q: *Describe King Arthur's confrontation with Mordred on the battlefield.*

A: In traditional battle formation, the two armies lined up on opposite ends of the battlefield. As father and son approached one another, one of Arthur's soldiers drew his sword to kill a snake that had fallen on his shoulder. Mordred's soldiers had been instructed to fight if a sword was drawn, so they immediately began to battle. The fighting lasted all day, and in the end, both the king and his son were mortally wounded.

Q: *Describe the circumstance of Arthur's death.*

A: After Arthur had killed Mordred, the exhausted king dropped onto the ground and clutched his own wounds. Arthur would not die until Sir Bors had thrown Excalibur back into the lake from which it had come. When at last Bors was able to part with the magical sword, Arthur's half-sister, Morgan Le Fay, came in a magical boat and took Arthur to Avalon, a mystical island far off to the west.

EXPERT COMMENTARY

In *Le Morte d'Arthur*, Mordred was left in charge of Camelot after King Arthur agreed to fight against Lancelot in France. The Arthurian scholar, Phyllis Ann Karr, is not sure why Malory chose to do this:

> Malory says Arthur did this because Mordred was his son, but this would seem to make Arthur surprisingly slow-witted about connecting Merlin's old prophecy and his own nightmare with Mordred, so it is my guess that Arthur may still have been unaware of the relationship and made Mordred his regent because Mordred was the last surviving brother of the King's favorite nephew Gawaine.[2]

Arthur was said to have died on the battlefield and been taken to Avalon on a magical boat by his half-sister, Morgan Le Fay. However, some scholars say he was only taken away until his wounds healed and that he would eventually return some time in the future. For this reason, some people believed that he had not been killed, and would someday return. Richard Barber states:

> He [Arthur] governed the realm of Britain for thirty-nine years in the power of his strength, the wisdom of his mind, the acuteness of his judgement, and through his renown in battle. In the fortieth year of his reign, he was destined to end his human lot. Therefore with Arthur dead, Constantine the son of Duke Cador, ascended to the British realm, etc. . . .[3]

It has been suggested that Arthur's final resting place at Avalon was perhaps a Celtic paradise where crops were produced without cultivation. Glastonbury, England, has been associated with Avalon, probably because Arthur's grave was purported to have been found there. Phyllis Ann Karr says:

> Nevertheless, Avilion [Avalon] comes across to me as a mystical center of repose, quite possibly Christian grafted onto Pagan with elements of the old creed remaining, and beneficent if a shade melancholy—a 'peaceable kingdom' of healing, sanctuary, and permanent, inviolate truce. Or perhaps, it might have been a gateway to the underworld of the dead.[4]

 GLOSSARY

allegiance—The obligation of support and loyalty to one's ruler, government, or country.

bard—An ancient Celtic poet that played a harp and sang verse.

chivalry—Respectful attention, especially toward women.

courtly love—A passionate—but illicit—love affair between one man and another man's wife.

damsel—An archaic term used for girl or maiden.

falconry—The training of falcons, which are birds of prey, to hunt.

fencing—The art or practice of attack and defense with the sword or foil.

feudalism—The economic, political, and social system in medieval Europe in which land was worked by serfs, or slaves, and held by feudal lords in exchange for military and other services given to overlords.

heraldry—A system of signs and family badges used on shields and flags from the Middle Ages onward; the art or science of coats of arms or genealogies.

jousting—Combat during which one knight on horseback charges another knight on horseback. Both riders carry lances and attempt to unseat each other.

knight—A soldier who fought on horseback during the European Middle Ages. Knights were ranked among the nobility.

lance—A long spear, almost always carried on horseback. Also, a unit in a medieval army led by a knight.

lord—An owner and head of a feudal estate and a member of the most powerful group in society. Nobles and the king himself were part of this group.

mail—Flexible armor made of interlinking iron rings, also known as chain mail.

Middle Ages—A term used by historians to describe the period between the end of the Roman Empire in A.D. 476 and the start of our modern world in about A.D. 1500.

moat—A deep, broad ditch dug around a fortress or castle, often filled with water, built to protect against enemy attack.

mortar—A mixture of sand and lime used to bind stones or bricks together.

overlord—A lord ranking above other lords in the feudal system.

page—A young boy who served a noble family as part of his training for knighthood.

peasant—A class of small farmers or farm laborers, especially in Europe and Asia.

Pentecost—A Christian festival celebrated on the seventh Sunday after Easter, celebrating the descent of the Holy Spirit upon the Apostles; also called Whitsunday, for the white garments worn by candidates for baptism.

scabbard—The sheath or casing that holds a sword.

serf—Originally a slave or an oppressed person without freedom; a person bound to his master's land in feudal servitude.

squire—A youth who trains for knighthood under the direction of an accomplished knight.

tournament—A mock battle arranged to amuse crowds and give training to knights.

vassal—Anyone who was granted land by a feudal lord in return for services.

⊞ CHAPTER NOTES ⊞

Preface

1. Richard White, ed., *King Arthur in Legend and History*. (New York: Routledge, 1997), p. xv.

2. Norris J. Lacy and Geoffrey Ashe, *The Arthurian Handbook*. (New York: Garland Publishing, Inc., 1997), pp. 1–2.

3. Ibid., pp. 10–11.

4. Ibid., p. 300.

5. F. E. Halliday, England: *A Concise History*. (London: Thames and Hudson Ltd., 1989), pp. 17-36.

6. *The Middle Ages: A Feudal Life*, http://www.learner.org/exhibits/middleages/feudal.html.

7. *Andreas Cappellanus' Rules of Courtly Love*, http://ebbs.english.vt.edu/mosser/classes/3014/rules.html

8. Norris J. Lacy and Geoffrey Ashe, *The Arthurian Handbook*. (New York: Garland Publishing, Inc., 1997), pp. 9–11.

9. Ibid., pp. 23–27.

10. Ibid., pp. 36–37.

11. Ibid., pp.128–130.

12. Interview with Geoffrey Ashe, http://panther.bsc.edu/arthur/ashe.html (March 22, 2002).

13. Norris J. Lacy and Geoffrey Ashe, *The Arthurian Handbook*. (New York: Garland Publishing, Inc., 1997), pp. 294–295.

Chapter 1. Young Arthur

1. *Cornwall*. Microsoft ® Encarta, 1993. Funk & Wagnall's Corporation.

2. Phyllis Ann Karr, *The Arthurian Companion*. (Canada: A Chaosium Book, 1997), pp. 330-335.

3. T. H. White, *The Once and Future King*. (New York: Ace Books, 1987), pp.1-209.

4. Sir Thomas Malory, *Le Morte d'Arthur*. (London, England: Cassel & Co., 2000), p.4.

5. Malory, p. 9.

6. Ibid.

7. Richard Barber, ed., *The Arthurian Legends*. (New York: The Boydell Press, 1996), p.2.

8. Karr, p. 332.

Chapter 2. The Magical Sword Excalibur

1. Richard Coghlan, *The Illustrated Encyclopaedia of Arthurian Legends*. (New York: Barnes & Noble, 1995), p. 100.

2. Sir Thomas Malory, *Le Morte d'Arthur*. (London, England: Cassel & Co., 2000), pp.46–47.

3. Phyllis Ann Karr, *The Arthurian Companion*. (Canada: A Chaosium Book, 1997), pp. 155.

4. Ibid.

5. Norris J. Lacy and Geoffrey Ashe, *The Arthurian Handbook*. (New York: Garland Publishing, Inc., 1997), p. 306.

Chapter 3. Morgan Le Fay

1. Ronan Coghlan, *The Illustrated Encyclopedia of Arthurian Legends*. (New York: Barnes & Noble Books, 1995), pp. 186–187.

2. Phyllis Ann Karr, *The Arthurian Companion*. (Canada: A Chaosium Book, 1997), pp. 341–345.

3. Ibid., p. 342.

4. Norris J. Lacy and Geoffrey Ashe, *The Arthurian Handbook*. (New York: Garland Publishing, Inc., 1997), p. 338.

Chapter 4. Gawain and the Green Knight

1. Norris J. Lacy and Geoffrey Ashe, *The Arthurian Handbook* (New York: Garland Publishing, Inc., 1997), pp. 126–128.

2. Burton Raffel, trans., *Sir Gawain and the Green Knight*. (New York: Penguin Putnam, Inc., 1970), pp. 49–125.

3. Ibid., p. 61.

4. Lacy and Ashe, p. 127.

5. Raffel, pp. 27–28.

Chapter 5. Percival

1. Norris J. Lacy and Geoffrey Ashe, *The Arthurian Handbook*. (New York: Garland Publishing, Inc., 1997), p. 68.

2. Phyllis Ann Karr, *The Arthurian Companion*. (Canada: A Chaosium Book, 1997), pp. 382–389.

3. Lacy and Ashe, p. 72.

4. Karr, p. 390.

Chapter 6. Lancelot and Guinevere

1. Richard White, ed., *King Arthur in Legend and History*. (New York: Routledge, 1997), p. 271.

2. Phyllis Ann Karr, *The Arthurian Companion*. (Canada: A Chaosium Book, 1997), pp. 268–276.

3. Norris J. Lacy and Geoffrey Ashe, *The Arthurian Handbook*. (New York: Garland Publishing, Inc., 1997), p.328.

4. Richard Barber, ed., *The Arthurian Legends*. (New York: The Boydell Press, 1996), p. 167.

Chapter 7. Galahad

1. Phyllis Ann Karr, *The Arthurian Companion*. (Canada: A Chaosium Book, 1997), p. 172.

2. Norris J. Lacy and Geoffrey Ashe, *The Arthurian Handbook*. (New York: Garland Publishing, Inc., 1997), p.307.

3. Lacy and Ashe, p. 307.

4. Roger Sherman Loomis, *Celtic Myth and Arthurian Romance*. (Chicago: Academy Chicago Publishers, 1995), pp. 140–141.

Chapter 8. Mordred

1. Phyllis Ann Karr, *The Arthurian Companion*. (Canada: A Chaosium Book, 1997), p. 338.

2. Ibid., pp. 339–341.

3. Karr, p. 340.

4. Georges Duby, ed. *A History of Private Life: Revelations of the Medieval World* (Cambridge, MA: Belknap Press, 1988) p. 339.

5. T. H. White, *The Book of Merlyn*, xxi.

Chapter 9. The Death of Arthur

1. Richard White, ed., *King Arthur in Legend and History*. (New York: Routledge, 1997), p. 290–297.

2. Phyllis Ann Karr, *The Arthurian Companion*. (Canada: A Chaosium Book, 1997), p. 340.

3. Richard Barber, ed., *The Arthurian Legends*. (New York: The Boydell Press, 1996), p. 32.

4. Karr, p. 54.

✛ FURTHER READING ✛

Aries, Philippe and Georges Duby, eds., *A History of Private Life: Revelations of the Medieval World*. Cambridge, Ma., The Belknap Press of Harvard University Press, 1988.

Barber, Richard, ed. *The Arthurian Legends*. Rochester, New York: The Boydell Press, 1996.

Brooks, Felicity, ed. *Tales of King Arthur*. London: Usborne Publishing Ltd., 1994.

Coghlan, Ronan. *The Illustrated Encyclopedia of Arthurian Legends*. New York: Barnes and Noble Books, 1995.

Crossley-Holland, Kevin. *The World of King Arthur and His Court*. New York: Dutton Children's Books, 1998.

Green, Roger Lancelyn. *King Arthur and his Knights of the Round Table*. London: Penguin Books, Ltd., 1994.

Halliday, F. E. *England: A Concise History*. London: Thames and Hudson Ltd., 1989.

Karr, Phyllis Ann. *The Arthurian Companion*. Canada: A Chaosium Book, 1997.

Lacy, Norris J. and Geoffrey Ashe. *The Arthurian Handbook*. New York: Garland Publishing, Inc., 1997.

Malory, Thomas Sir. *Le Morte d'Arthur*. John Matthews, ed. London: Cassell & Co., 2000.

Markale, Jean. *King of the Celts*. Rochester, Vt.: Inner Traditions, 1994.

McCoy, Edain. *Celtic Myth and Magic*. St. Paul: Llewellyn Press, 1995.

Morris, Gerald. *The Savage Damsel and the Dwarf*. Boston: Houghton, Mifflin, 2000.

Morris, Gerald. *The Squire, His Knight, and His Lady*. Boston: Houghton, Mifflin, 1999.

Raffel, Burton, trans., *Sir Gawain and the Green Knight*. New York: Penguin Putnam Inc., 1970.

Steele, Philip. *The Medieval World*. New York: Kingfisher Publications, 2000.

Talbott, Hudson. *Lancelot*. New York: Morrow Junior Books., 1999.

Tyler, Jenny, ed. *Tales of King Arthur*. London: Usborne Publishing Ltd., 1994.

White, Richard, ed. *King Arthur in Legend and History*. New York: Routledge, 1998.

White, T. H. *The Sword in the Stone*. New York: G. P. Putnam's Sons, 1963.

White, T. H. *The Once and Future King*. New York: Ace Books, 1987.

White, T. H. *The Book of Merlyn*. Austin, Texas: University of Texas Press, 1977.

INTERNET ADDRESSES

Arthurian Resources on the Internet
<http://jan.ucc.nau.edu/~jjd23/arthur/Arthur_Old/general.html>

The Quest
<http://www.uidaho.edu/student_orgs/arthurian_legend/welcome.html>

✥ INDEX ✥